T0061939

PENGUIN BUSINESS
TRANSFORM

Chandramouli Venkatesan (1968–2020) was a corporate veteran with over twenty-six years of experience in the industry. He has worked with Asian Paints, Cadbury/Mondelez, MIRC Electronics/Onida and Pidilite. He has served in various senior capacities, including chief executive officer and managing director. While the bulk of his professional life has been in business and P&L leadership roles, there was a three-year period when he did a cross-functional stint as HR head for Cadbury India which further developed his understanding of what makes people successful.

Chandramouli was a keen golfer and sports enthusiast, and believed in holding his life in balance. This, coupled with his sense of values and spirituality, led him to believe that every person must impact society positively. He has conducted numerous speaking sessions that have benefited over 1000 people, and mentored and guided many others to be successful in their careers.

He is the author of *Catalyst* and *Get Better at Getting Better*.

ADVANCE PRAISE FOR THE BOOK

'There are many books on leadership but the reason *Transform* should be read by all corporate employees with a desire to move up the corporate ladder and management students in preparation for their corporate careers is that Mouli himself, first, an effective manager and in later years, an inspirational leader, writes this book based on his experiences and offers practical and usable guidance. Most leaders make the mistake of not managing whilst leading, and most managers make the mistake of not leading at all. Mouli expands on this important aspect which can increase your effectiveness quotient substantially'—Sam Balsara, chairman, Madison World

'Mouli's insightful final book reminds us that the difference between good and great managers is their ability to both lead and manage. This book is a treasure trove of anecdotes and practical tips on how to do what is seldom taught—making other people successful. A must-read for all those who aspire to lead. Keep it close by for reference repeatedly—as you lead your teams to success'—Bharat Puri, managing director, Pidilite Industries

'Mouli's ability to observe, draw insights and convert that to practical models for improvement is exceptional. In this book, he very ably brings out the difference between being a manager and a leader—and the need to practise both as you grow in your career. The self-reflection will help you become more effective—helping you to maximize your potential—while making an even bigger impact on your organization. A must-read if you want to transform yourself and become the best YOU possible'—Anand Kripalu, managing director and global CEO, EPL Ltd, and ex-managing director and CEO, Diageo India and Cadbury India

'*Transform* as a book reminds me a bit of Mouli himself—always focusing on people around him, always looking at ways to maximize their potential, being a part of that endeavour. It is a book that will truly be of great help to any manager who wishes to achieve success through their people. Not only does it talk about the theory and concepts related to this, it also gives a great practical way to achieve this . . . an insightful read'—Harsh Mariwala, founder and chairman, Marico

'Mouli has written an appropriate book on people management in an era dominated by digital skills. People management is about the context, and a leader who is "self-aware" manages this well. Transform your self-awareness with this book'—Shiv Shivakumar, group executive president, corporate strategy and business development, Aditya Birla Group

'How do you help your people grow and, in doing so, grow yourself? As someone who has been both CEO and HR head, Mouli is uniquely placed to speak about this. Clear, simple and actionable, this is a must-read for both aspiring and current leaders'—Ranjan Banerjee, dean and professor, marketing, BITS School of Management

'When a book is written in simple human terms, it helps humans to find parallels in all aspects of life. I found mine in cricket—if you're a captain, your job is to lead the team and manage the players, to get the best out of them—that is how you develop future captains. Read this simple book and find your own parallel, in your family, friends, at work and in society. The book will remind you to do a daily exercise, no matter how fit you think you are'—Piyush Pandey, chief creative officer worldwide and executive chairman India, Ogilvy

'If you want to fast-track your way to becoming a better leader and manager, this is the book to read—and read again. The practical tools and techniques will help you master the skills to become more effective. Mouli's personal wisdom and wealth of experiences make the book all the more compelling'—Vivek Gambhir, CEO, boAt Lifestyle

'This is a compelling read, suitable for professionals who truly want to invest in building their careers. Mouli's framing of people management skills in a simple and practical way can be a guide to any manager or leader at any point in their careers. With this third book, Mouli successfully completes a terrific trilogy on managing careers'—Deepak Iyer, president, Mondelez International India

'*Transform* is the jewel in the crown of Mouli's trilogy. This book truly challenges and compels the readers to view the traditional concepts of leadership and management from the opposite plane. As usual, Mouli has also provided a nice, useful toolkit to help the practitioner experience the concepts. Though this is his last book, it will last forever for those who get transformed by reading this book'—Annaswamy Vaidheesh, former managing director and vice president, GSK South Asia and Johnson & Johnson Medical

'Chandramouli's book provides a thorough exploration of the art of successful management. A must-read for managers and aspiring leaders, *Transform* is a pertinent guide on how managers can shift from simply managing to truly leading. The book expertly draws on the inextricable link between people skills and leadership, offering actionable advice on how to leverage the skills involved in managing people to grow a successful team'—Leena Nair, CHRO, Unilever, and member of the Unilever Leadership Executive

'*Transform* by Chandramouli Venkatesan curates an epitome of simplicity, woven in the milieu of the truths of practicality, the incredible art of "creating a breakthrough in one's leadership". The book leaves you amazed, the way it amplifies people management as an entrenched pillar in embracing the steps of a transformational leader and how to leave a legacy, impacting and touching people. Chandramouli, while busting the myths of "leader" and "manager", tables his intrinsic and profound understanding by bringing six key, simple and practical concepts to elevate the manager and the leader in you. The lucidity of the flow of concepts takes you on a guided path by which you not only absorb the nuances of the various concepts, but truly can draw an action plan to elevate your career and coach yourself to be the "next gen transformational leader"'—Amit Syngle, managing director and CEO, Asian Paints

Transform

the ultimate guide to

lead~~er~~ and manage~~r~~

From the bestselling author of

catalyst

CHANDRAMOULI
VENKATESAN

BUSINESS

An imprint of Penguin Random House

PENGUIN BUSINESS

USA | Canada | UK | Ireland | Australia
New Zealand | India | South Africa | China

Penguin Business is part of the Penguin Random House group of companies
whose addresses can be found at global.penguinrandomhouse.com

Published by Penguin Random House India Pvt. Ltd
4th Floor, Capital Tower 1, MG Road,
Gurugram 122 002, Haryana, India

First published in Penguin Business by Penguin Random House India 2021

ISBN 9780670096374

Typeset in Aldine401 BT by Manipal Technologies Limited, Manipal
Printed at Thomson Press India Ltd, New Delhi

www.penguin.co.in

To Mouli—who lived, learnt and taught to the fullest and left a huge mark on us all

Contents

Contents

SECTION 3

SECTION 4

Foreword

Greetings, readers!

My father, Chandramouli Venkatesan, was a man with a great vision—one of a long line of books that he intended to write, to help people navigate the complexities of career and life. I fondly remember him excitedly telling me his plans for retirement and how he already had his next seven books planned out in his head.

He was never in it for the money, but for a concept he stood behind; one he outlined in his first book *Catalyst* as well. The concept is one of return on investment (ROI) to society and the people around him. He always believed that the way he could give back to society in the most impactful manner—a way that would maximize his ROI—would be to teach others and help them navigate the challenges of work and life. And one of the most effective ways he chose to do that was through his books. *Catalyst* was his first success; it showed him that what he was trying to achieve was real and significant. *Get Better at Getting Better* was an attempt to go into greater depth on one of the many lessons he wanted to convey. And he had many, many more planned ahead. Unfortunately, that dream will never come to fruition.

Last year, my father lost his life to pancreatic cancer. In a year where the world was battling COVID-19, and many families struggled through loss and difficulty, he too was taken away from us. A man who had the intelligence, talent, sheer determination and willpower to change things—and a love for the people and the world around him—was lost to those who loved him back.

While the diagnosis hit him and our family hard, my father was never the type to just sit around worrying about things that were out of his control. Instead, he decided to focus all his efforts on only two things—managing his health, and writing this book.

And oh, how he threw himself into the task! He would disappear into his room for hours on end, typing away at his laptop. It kept him occupied for months, and I think writing this book really gave him a purpose, a reason to try harder each day. He had good days and bad ones, but he never gave up on this book. He turned to experts for advice and friends for support through the journey. He started planning the publishing timelines and creative decisions for marketing the book. Within record time, barely four months from the day he had been diagnosed, he completed a first draft of the book.

He had every intention of seeing this book through to the end, but life had other plans. His health turned for the worse and we lost him quickly after that.

My father was the person I respected and loved most in the world. He was more than a parent—he was my teacher, my mentor, my supporter, and a role model so very integral to who I have become today. In a way, I have followed in his footsteps in my own journey in life and my career as well.

As a tribute to this wonderful man, I was determined to ensure the publishing of this book—to honour and keep alive his memory, to never let his hard work during the tail end of his life be wasted.

I have had heaps of help from so many older and wiser people whom I could never thank enough for all they have done for me, my father, and this book. And in the course of this journey, this book has become mine as much as it was his. I have read and edited and re-read every line of the book. I have changed and added and modified. I have looked at book titles and covers and marketing plans. Through it all, I have learnt so much—both from the content of this book and the life lessons experienced during such an extensive personal project. I feel that, in some sense, this book was intended as a final gift, certainly for all his beloved readers, but also as a learning opportunity for me. A gift of love and learning, a gift that he wanted to last forever.

While I may be positively biased, the book is a very real and clear perspective of what many of us face in our lives when interacting with other people. While he puts forth his arguments from the lens of someone in a corporate career, I truly believe that anyone, everyone, can learn to apply these principles in their daily lives. How many of us really understand what makes others tick? Do we really try to find those answers, or do we content ourselves with our assumptions of others? While we may instinctively know some of this in the back of our heads, most of us have never figured out how to put those ideas into action. It's my belief that reading this book will really give you the tools to deciphering others, and teach you how to interact and work with them in a productive manner.

I can only hope that his final work, this book—*Transform*—is able to help you navigate your life a little bit better. If it does, I, and so many others, will consider our hard work to have paid off. Most importantly, it would make his last act on Earth one of being able to help others through his ideas and experiences. I cannot think of a more fitting end to a man with a mission—a legacy that he will always be remembered by.

—Prerana Chandramouli

Introduction

I completed my chemical engineering from A.C. Tech, Anna University, Chennai in 1989. Subsequently, I did my MBA from XLRI, Jamshedpur in 1991. Thereafter, in a career spanning nearly thirty years, I have largely worked in business-facing roles; be they marketing or sales or P&L leadership roles. However, I ended up doing one cross-functional stint in HR, where, between 2007 and 2010, I was the head of HR for Cadbury India (now Mondelez India). Whenever I get to something new, I always like to start with the very basics. And when I got to HR after sixteen years of sales, marketing and business, the first and most basic question I asked myself was:

'How does HR help a company succeed?'

I have done a lot of marketing and if you asked me, 'How does marketing help a company succeed?', I would have had a clear reply. I would say marketing helps a company succeed through branding and innovation. If marketing does a great job of brand-building, leveraging all consumer touchpoints and the consumer journey; if marketing does a great job of innovation and new offerings, then the company will succeed. If marketing does a poor job of branding and innovation, then the company is unlikely to.

When I tried to find a similarly simple and clear answer to the question, 'How does HR help a company succeed?', I struggled. There were quite a few varying answers within the HR fraternity itself, ranging from talent to culture to engagement and so on and so forth. It took me a fair while to distil the answer in my head, but I finally landed on an answer that made sense to me. I said, **'HR makes a company successful by making the people in the company successful'.** If a lot of people in a company succeed, then that company will automatically do well; and if very few people in a company succeed, then that company is unlikely to be successful. Hence, the role of HR for me was to 'make people successful'.

While it was a challenging process in itself to arrive at the answer, only after I had reached it did I realize that what I had solved was the easy part. The difficult part remained—how to make people successful? The path to good brand-building is not a black hole; there is a lot of science, information and expertise available on it, which one can rely upon to drive efforts in the right direction. However, on the topic of 'how to make people successful', I found that the information and science was not that easy to access and assimilate. While there are countless self-improvement books and formulaic ones, I was not convinced that those offered the kind of information I was looking for. They all add value in different ways, but it may be difficult for a person to absorb all that value scattered across different sources.

I decided to search for the answer myself. In the years that followed, from 2007 till around 2015, I kept observing those who succeeded and the reasons for their success as much as I followed those who did not. I observed people in my workplace, my friends, relatives, batchmates, etc. in other companies as well. With all these observations, I tried to piece together a comprehensive success toolkit in my mind, and find an answer to my question—how to make people successful?

At the end of this exercise, I found that successful people are very effective in managing the following four levers:

1. Getting better continuously
2. Career management
3. Life management
4. People management

Getting better continuously is about how effectively you are improving your skills, capabilities, judgement, decision-making, communication, etc. It is about whether you are able to grow rapidly as a professional.

Career management is about the strategy and decisions you take to manage your career. A particularly important insight is that most people succeed in the first half of their careers and very few do so in the second. Hence, a career management strategy is needed to ensure that you win where it matters—the second half of your career.

Life management is about your life as opposed to your work; how you live your life can be a great driver to how successful you can be. It is about whether you are growing rapidly as a person.

People management, the last lever, is the focus of this book and I shall cover it in more detail in the coming pages and chapters.

The first book I wrote in the space of career success was *Catalyst,* published in 2018. It largely focused on career management and life management, albeit with a reasonable slice on getting better. Having written *Catalyst*, I still felt that getting better and continuous self-improvement was too important a success lever to just be a sub-part of one book covering several topics. It deserved a full book in itself; and that is how I wrote my second book, *Get Better at Getting Better*, which was published in 2019. This book, which is currently in your hands, *Transform,* seeks to cover people management. Hence, in effect, with these three books, all the four levers of success are well covered. There is some overlap between the books as these are interrelated levers. Hence, people who have read my previous books may notice some similarities, but they arise simply because these are not isolated topics, but are closely connected. Those who read all three books together will obtain the comprehensive success toolkit that I want to provide those who are looking to succeed in their careers and lives.

This book, titled *Transform—the Ultimate Guide to Lead & Manage*, focuses on people management, which I believe is a very important pillar from among the four levers of success. I prefer to call the lever 'people management' and not leadership or managing people, etc. That is because leadership and managing are the means, while the end impact is what they do to *people*, i.e., how they transform them in their careers and as people. We need to keep in mind that it is not about what we do, but about the impact it creates on people who are in our sphere. Of course, the book will cover how to lead and manage but from a perspective of how it impacts those we lead and manage. In a nutshell, this book aims to transform you into a great people manager so that you can find yourself among the ranks of the great leaders we all aspire towards. This is why I decided the name the book so—reading this book will help you transform the people around you, yourself and your success in your career, all through learning how best to lead and manage those people.

As you are aware, there are thousands of leadership books jostling for space. I have had the opportunity to read a few and I wanted to make sure that my book is not just another leadership and management book. As I read them, I realized that there are two broad kinds of books—the first kind talk about high-level leadership concepts which may sound good but could be difficult to implement practically; the second kind go deeper into a micro topic and do a fantastic job of explaining both theory and implementation, but do not serve as comprehensive tools because they are niche. My effort, therefore, has been to create a leadership and management book which is comprehensive, and covers all the important concepts while giving practical implementation techniques for each. I have tried to do all this in a quick 280-page read. To do it in 280 pages has also meant that I have had to ruthlessly prioritize only the most important concepts. There are likely to be concepts of leadership and management outside of what is in this book that may be good concepts in themselves. But I do think that even if readers implement only this prioritized package of concepts as outlined in this book, then they would be well on their way to success.

When I developed the content for this book, I first converted it into a development programme called Lead & Manage, and I used to run it for companies. Conducting these workshops allowed me to sharpen my insights, understand the challenges and questions that arise as well as make it practical for people to apply it in their daily lives. The feedback and learning from running that programme have been built into the writing of this book and hopefully, you will find it insightful yet practical.

As you go through this book, you will find some chapters that talk about exercises you will need to do and space has been provided for those. Please do not skip those exercises, as they are meant to help you connect the concepts being explained to your reality. Each reader of this book is bound to have a different reality and it is only these exercises that will connect this book to your unique reality and make the book truly practical and actionable. A lot of people tend to skip such exercises due to various reasons. My sincere request to you is to do the exercises with diligence and all your focus. This book is a practical guide to leadership and managing people, and by skipping the exercises, you will be losing out on the opportunity to try the lessons out.

This book has four sections.

Section 1: This section focuses on introducing the core concept of *Transform*—the concept of leading and managing. It will also present a series of exercises to open your mind and make you more self-aware as a leader and a manager, as well as potentially identify important areas for improvement.

Section 2: This section will focus on becoming great at managing with an emphasis on the direct team you manage. The three important concepts that we will cover here are—how to manage a team member for *performance,* how to manage a team member as a person (what I call how to manage the *performer* not the *performance)* and lastly, how to go beyond managing individuals to managing teams.

Section 3: This section will focus on becoming great at leading. We will deal with two important approaches here—*leading by doing* and *leading by being*. As is evident, 'leading by doing' will focus on a set of specific things you must do over and above your day-to-day work to lead well, while 'leading by being' focuses on how you are as a leader when you do your day-to-day work and how you can leverage that to lead well.

Section 4: This section will be about creating action plans. It will help you arrive at an action plan for yourself and allow you to develop a practical and implementable plan towards becoming a great leader and manager.

As my readers are aware, I write my books predominantly based on my thoughts and learnings, and I do not do active research for the books. My attempt is to always share practical learnings and experiences that I have amassed and hence make it useful for people as opposed to being high on content but not being practical and usable. This lack of research does mean that what I write is not scientifically validated; it is based more on my belief system and my point of view. So do read the book with that disclaimer and if, in any area, your beliefs are staunchly different from what is written in the book, by all means stick to them. People management through leadership and management is not a narrow, one-dimensional science and different methods can work for different people. May your impact on people be positive and meaningful and may you become the leader and the manager that you are capable of becoming! Happy reading.

SECTION 1

1

Leaders and Managers

In recent times, I have been watching with great interest, and at times, part amusement, the growing chorus on how a 'leader' is great and how a 'manager' is bad. Open up LinkedIn and there are so many posts comparing leaders and managers. Some of the posts that particularly caught my eye were the kind which had the imagery of a manager standing behind his team and pushing them or whipping them to perform, while a leader is shown standing ahead and leading his team in an inspiring way. Others that come to mind readily are quotes like 'Managers give you a task while leaders provide you with a vision and direction' or 'Managers get you to perspire while leaders inspire'. One could write a whole book on this—the cartoons, memes and quotes that glorify the leader and vilify the manager. Each one of these, in a way, exhorts us to stop being a manager and try to become a leader.

I have also noticed that this is a relatively recent phenomenon, possibly in the last decade or so. I have not seen so much vilification of the manager and glorification of a leader in the time I grew up as a relative newbie in the corporate world. It set me thinking on why this has become so widespread in the last ten to fifteen years to the extent that the word 'manager' and 'manage' are actually becoming bad words. My most inspired guess towards this 'why' is that most people have a problem with their bosses—their managers; a boss is never perfect in the eyes of the subordinate. And to compound that, the world has enough bad managers and bosses as well. With the proliferation of social media, there has been an outpouring of sorts from people on how bad their managers are and the best way to show that is by comparing them with the symbol of perfection—the mythical perfect leader. The grass is always greener on the other side. And so, the memes, cartoons and quotable quotes, in my opinion, stem from this yearning that people have for better bosses and managers.

The other potential explanation is the growth of the leadership development industry. It is a lot sexier to do a leadership development programme than a manager development programme. For the same content, if you call the programme 'leadership development' instead of 'manager development', you could possibly charge a higher rate. I also conduct leadership development programmes and sometimes, I wonder if I too contribute to this phenomenon. From the participants' perspective too, it is a lot cooler to say that they are attending a leadership development programme than a manager development workshop. Many companies, as a part of their learning and development programmes, have multiple leadership development programmes and possibly not even a single manager development programme, despite the fact that the population of managers in that company might be quite large.

Whatever the reason may be, the fact remains that in the popular narrative today, a leader is great and a manager/boss is not so great. If we see it through to its logical end, what would the implications be? Does it mean that everyone should become a leader and no one should be a manager? Does it mean that bosses should always be inspiring and no one should ever crack the whip if required? Does it mean that vision is the only thing that matters and task orientation should completely be given up? Obviously, leadership and the art of managing people are not as simplistic as this. There are two myths we must bust in this context.

1. The first myth to bust with regard to the current narrative is its one-dimensional nature. It pivots the debate as a leader versus a manager. I believe it is not 'versus' but an 'and'; it is leader *and* manager. That is the right way to look at this game. If you want to be great at people management—and in the introduction we spoke about how people management is foundational to being successful in your career—then you have to master the 'and'. You have to be both a leader and a manager; no one can afford to be just one of the two. The junior-most manager can't afford to be just a manager, they need to be a leader as well. Similarly, the senior-most leader cannot afford to be just a leader, they need to be good managers as well.

2. The second myth associated with the current narrative is the emphasis it places on the person and the title rather than the action. So, if you are called a manager then you are expected to manage and, if your position is that of a leader, then you are expected to lead. So, your title of leader or manager dictates the role you are expected to play, and implies that you can only be one of the two, not both. It also perpetuates this myth that once a person is denoted as and called a 'leader', then everything they do is automatically leadership—even micro, insignificant actions of theirs are hailed as leadership; even managerial actions of theirs start getting called leadership. Vice versa, once a person is denoted as a 'manager', then all their actions are considered managerial; and even if they take some leadership actions, they end up being viewed as managerial actions. Hence, this narrative says that whether you lead or whether you manage is primarily determined by the title and position you have—if you are a leader, then you must lead and if you are a manager, you must manage.

Hence, the two broad myths that they keep perpetuating are:

1. You are either a leader or a manager
2. Your title and your position determine whether you should lead or focus on managerial actions

The way to break out of this is to acknowledge that everyone has to act as both—a leader and a manager. It is not important whether you are a leader or a manager, what is important is whether you are leading *and* managing.

To become good at people management, here is what I want you to do—do not focus on who you are but on what you do—your actions and your behaviour.
Ask yourself:

a) how good am I at leading?
b) how good am I at managing? and
c) what does it take for me to get even better at leading and managing people?

The more you focus on what you do—your actions—and the less you focus on who you are—your title—the more effective you will be at people management.

Leade~~r~~

and ~~or~~

Manage~~r~~

This visual brings to life the two key shifts that I have been referring to till now in this chapter for you to become great at people management.

Shift 1: It is an 'and' and not an 'or'. Everyone has to do both. The junior-most manager must know that they don't just have to manage but also lead, and the

senior-most leader must realize that they must not just
lead but also manage.

Shift 2: It is not about the title or the position; it is not
about whether you are called a leader or a manager. Instead,
it is about what you do, your actions, your behaviour and
your decisions on how to lead and manage.

To focus on the actions—to *lead* and *manage* people with
impact—it is important to understand the definition of
these two terms. The terms lead, leading, leadership,
leader, manage, manager, managing, etc. have been
floating about forever but a simple search will not reveal
straightforward, precise, actionable definitions for these.
Often, when people would return after attending a
leadership development programme, I would ask them to
tell me the definition of leadership. As you can expect, the
answers were many and highly varied. Some would say it
is about providing a vision and direction to people; some
would say it is about being authentic; some would say
it is about inspiring people and creating self-belief. You
can see a pattern in the answers. Most of the answers are
about what you do as a leader and some of the different
sub-facets of leadership. These answers don't focus on the
purpose of leading and leadership in an integrated way.

You must wonder why it is so important to define these
precisely. After all, these are complex topics and it seems
fair to expect a multitude of definitions and explanations.
The reason why I focus on a sharp definition is to make it
actionable for improvement. If you accept the definition
of leadership as providing vision and direction, then you

can focus on improving that facet, but would that be enough to make you lead effectively? If you accept the definition as inspiring and creating self-belief in people, then you can focus on improving that aspect, but would that be enough to make you a great leader?

Defining it through multiple sub-facets limits our strategy to improve our leadership abilities, and also does not get us to an ideal final outcome. Hence, I prefer a good, sharp definition that is based on the purpose— why do we lead and why do we manage; and what are the outcomes we expect. It was quite a challenge to get to these definitions—they are just a few lines—but possibly the most challenging part of writing this book. However, finally, I reached a set of definitions that I feel comfortable with. So here they are:

Managing: The art of impacting people while being directly involved

Leading: The art of impacting people without being directly involved

As you read the definitions, it will immediately become clear that these are actionable. You know that to become better at leading, you have to grow your impact where you are not directly involved. A general becomes a great leader when the troops in the trenches are positively impacted by him without him even meeting them once. A CEO becomes a great leader when a person in the factory is inspired to produce the best quality goods despite the CEO never having directly engaged with them.

You become good at managing when your decisions on an issue you are directly involved with are clear; your actions are sharp and precise, and the people with whom you are directly involved on that subject are actively and positively engaged with you and your actions.

Let us take a few examples to understand this better. Examples of managing are a dime a dozen and a lot of our time every day goes in activities we are directly involved in with people. For e.g., during the preparation for the launch of Oreo Biscuits in 2011, I would have meetings with my team on the progress of the project on a regular basis; make decisions on packaging design and pricing, work on the advertising, test and validate the product, etc. These are examples of managing as I was directly involved in each of these decisions with my team. I now want to give you a 'leading' example for the same product. As we finally got everything ready and were getting close to launch, we had to get the frontline sales managers to prepare launch plans for their respective markets and territories. I was not going to be directly involved with them in preparing the launch plan for each territory, which is something that they would do themselves—I would possibly not even know what plans they had prepared. But I wanted to create an impact without being directly involved in their planning. So, I stood before the group of frontline sales managers and said the following:

> *'There are very few brands in the world like Oreo, brands which have a global legacy of over a hundred years. Maybe other brands like this are Coca-Cola and Cadbury, etc. These brands can be launched only once—once it is launched, it stays*

launched. Once a Coca-Cola is launched in India, subsequent generations of people working in that company will never have the privilege of launching Coca-Cola again. Most people go through an entire career of forty years never having launched a brand of such proportions. Today, you as a team, have this opportunity, to launch Oreo—a truly historic brand with over a hundred-year global legacy and one of the most loved brands in the world. And this chance will come only once in your life, you will never launch Oreo again. You will possibly never ever launch a brand of Oreo's pedigree again. It is a privilege you have and subsequent generations of people in our company will look back at this team as the people who launched Oreo. It is an opportunity for each one of you to leave behind a legacy with Oreo in your markets. As you prepare the launch plans, remember this and let it be the best-ever new product launch plan you ever made, and let this be the best executed new product launch ever.'

Now this was an example of leading. The activity in question was the preparation of territorial plans by frontline managers for Oreo's launch in respective markets. It was an activity that I would not be directly involved in; I was not even going to review their plans after they were prepared. Yet, I wanted to make an impact without being involved and I did that in this case by inspiring them. This was part of my leadership contribution for the launch—the art of impacting people without being directly involved in the activity.

Hopefully, you have got a good sense of managing and leading through the Oreo example I described above. These examples are where managing and leading are both different activities. There is an interesting third type of action you can take, where a single activity has both managing and leading impacts. Let us take an example of this. Imagine a factory production line and a serious problem with a piece of equipment. The factory head, Sumit, along with the maintenance head, Rakesh and production head, Ayushi are standing on the shop floor discussing the problem and identifying a probable solution. Hence, Sumit is directly involved in the discussion and in arriving at the solution. After this, Sumit calls the group of workmen who work on that machine on a day-to-day basis; people who know how the machine works, but don't know the technical and engineering aspects of it. He then describes to them what he thinks the problem is; the solution they have arrived at and asks them for their opinion. The workmen give their feedback and he listens to it, building some of it into the solution.

Now, if you look at the above example from Sumit's perspective, the situation has both managing and leading dimensions to it. The fact that there is a problem with an equipment which is impacting production is a situation requiring 'managing' and Sumit is directly involved in solving that problem and making required decisions. However, his action of calling the workmen to ask their opinion can create an indirect leading impact. It has an indirect impact on other managers whereby they could seek workmen's opinions on problems in the future. Sumit is not directly telling Rakesh and Ayushi that they must seek workmen's opinions in the future, but by his behaviour and action, he is modelling the culture he seeks to create in the factory. This is an example of leading impact. The more Sumit keeps building this culture, the higher the chances of an indirect impact on people in the factory to adopt this culture of involving workmen in solutions.

In effect, there are typically three kinds of situations:

1. Purely managing situations
2. Purely leading situations
3. Situations which have opportunity for both

The Oreo examples gave you an idea of a purely managing situation and a purely leading situation. Sumit's example gives you an idea of a situation that involves both managing and leading. This also helps recognize a continuum from poor leadership to great leadership. In that continuum, poor leaders are those who are only focused on managing situations. The bulk of their attention is focused only on people and things they are directly involved in—they do not take out the time to consciously do a set of deliberate things to lead; they seldom involve themselves in leading, they are content with managing. A better leader is a person who, while staying directly involved in managerial aspects, takes time out for purely leading actions so as to create impact beyond the people they are directly involved with. Those we perceive as great leaders are the ones who effectively manage situations where they are directly involved; who take time out for purely leading situations and most importantly, use every single managing situation to also create a leading impact. They are being managers and leaders all the time, not just one at a time. The trick to becoming a great leader lies there.

The senior-most leaders in companies, including the CEO, do take some time out for pure leading actions. However, the majority of their time goes into situations they are directly involved in, i.e., managing situations. They are involved in complex decisions like strategy, M&A, allocating capital and making key talent decisions. Hence, the trick to being a great leader is not to reduce the amount of time spent in pure managerial actions and increase the time allocated for pure leadership actions, but to use every single managing situation to also have a leadership impact. Later in this book, we will talk about *leadership by doing* and *leadership by being* and that should bring this concept to life for readers.

Another way of thinking about this is the 'what' and the 'how' of managing. In a situation where you are directly involved, there is a set of things you do which we can call the 'what'. At the same time, there is a 'how', which is the way you are doing those things. As you solve a problem through direct personal involvement with some people, are you talking in an aggressive, authoritative tone or are you speaking in a measured and open tone? Are you listening to different points of view (POVs) even if they are different from what you might think or are you only pushing your own solution? These 'hows' impact the people who are with you in that situation indirectly and eventually their behaviour over a period of time—a leading impact. You might get to the right answer from a managing sense to solve that problem, but the 'how' will determine whether the leading impact you have is positive or negative.

I hope that cements the very core concepts of what managing and leading are. Managing is the art of impacting people while being directly involved and leading is the art of impacting people without being directly involved. You can choose to do these independently and separate the managing and leading actions, but the best in the game are able to do both together.

This brings us to another important question—what is the relative importance of managing and leading? Does everyone have to be excellent at both to be good at people management and become successful? If someone is very good at managing and has a great impact where they are directly involved but is not too good at leading and creating impact beyond where they are involved, would they become successful? Similarly, if someone is very good at pure leading situations, in inspiring and leading, but not too good at situations where they have to be directly involved and manage, would they become successful?

I believe being good at managing is the base—it is a necessary but not sufficient condition. You have to be good at managing people who are working directly for you—you have to be good at having a positive impact in situations you are directly involved in. A large percentage of our time does go in situations where we are directly involved and if we are going to be bad at this, then there is little chance of being successful. Even for senior leaders who are excellent in leading situations, at delivering inspiring speeches and in making people feel comfortable in their presence, managing is a crucial skill. If they continuously get what they are directly involved in wrong; if they don't manage their direct teams well, they are unlikely to succeed. We have all seen such leaders who, for the first few months, look like they say the right things and have the right behavioural traits, but slowly, these get chipped off because they are poor at directly managing situations where they directly involved. On the other hand, someone who is good at managing but not so good at leading will still have reasonable success as long as they are not dysfunctional in their lack of leadership. Again, we have seen such CXOs who are not inspiring; who may not impact the culture and behaviour of the organization but still seem successful because they are effective in what they are directly involved in. So, in a sense, managing is the base. Managing your direct team well and having a positive impact where you are directly involved is mandatory; for without that, there is very little chance of being successful.

Leading is the accelerator or the decelerator to this. If someone has the base capability of managing and is also good at leading, then they will see accelerated success. And the opposite is also true—if someone is good at managing but has negative leading impact, then they will see their success getting decelerated. Hence, if you want to truly multiply your success, then you also have to focus on being good at impacting people where you are not directly involved. This book will also progress in this order—we will deal with the base first, i.e., managing followed by leading. The managing section will equip you with concepts and tools to manage your direct team well, impacting those people and actions you are directly involved with. Once we have done that, we will progress to concepts and tools for leading effectively in the latter half of the book.

Leader~~r~~

and ~~or~~

Manage~~r~~

As we revisit this visual, I want you to think of the word 'universal'. There is a universal application of this:

1. Every situation has the opportunity to do both. The universe of situations you face is your canvas to lead and manage.
2. Every person has the opportunity to do both. Everyone in the universe can both lead and manage.

We discussed how people management is one among the four pillars of success in the introduction along with getting better, career management and life management. If you want to be good at people management, then you must embrace this universality of the opportunity. Whatever be your title, try and become good at both leading and managing and, in every situation you face, try and do both—try and have both a direct impact and an indirect impact.

Chapter summary:

1. The current popular narrative glorifies the leader and paints the manager as a villain. If you want to be successful in people management, you must not fall into the trap of this narrative.

2. The narrative positions it as leader 'or' manager. It is not an 'or' but an 'and'. Everyone must strive to be both. The narrative also emphasizes the title and the position—what you are called does not matter, what you do matters. Being effective in leading *and* managing is more important than whether you are called a leader or a manager.

3. Understanding the definitions of leading and managing is important to be able to make any strategy to improve yourself in either. The definitions I like are:

   a. *Managing: The art of impacting people while being directly involved*
   b. *Leading: The art of impacting people without being directly involved*

4. There are three kinds of situations—purely managing situations, purely leading situations and situations where you can do both. Great leaders are those who use every managing situation to also have an indirect impact, a leading impact. They do this by not just focusing on the 'what', but also on the 'how', which is their behaviour in that managing situation.

5. Being good at managing is the base. Without being good at what you are directly involved in—being good at managing your direct team, you have a limited chance of success. Leading is the accelerator or the decelerator. Someone who is good in managing can either accelerate their career by having positive leading impact or decelerate their career by having negative leading impact.

6. Think of the word 'universal'. Every person has an opportunity to do both and every situation has the opportunity to do both.

2

Self-Awareness, Setting Standards and Authentic Leadership

There was once an individual, Nilesh, who I observed when I was collecting insights for this book. Nilesh, by any standard, could be easily classified as a bad manager and leader. He was hyper sharp, blessed with high IQ, had a tremendous understanding of the business and numbers, and possessed educational pedigree and past experience of the highest order. He had a lot of things going for him except that the people he managed disliked him (I am using a milder word, hated might be more appropriate). He was a poor and dysfunctional manager of people and a poor leader for the wider organization. Eventually, over time, so much of this feedback was passed on to the higher-ups that he was finally asked to leave the company. Not because he was not smart and did not know the business, but because he could not lead and manage well.

This made me reflect and ask the question—how can someone who is so smart not know that he is such a terrible manager? There can be only two explanations:

1. Either he intentionally wanted to be a terrible manager and leader and enjoyed managing his people poorly and making their lives miserable.

Or

2. He was simply not self-aware that he was such a poor manager and was under the misconception that he was good at leading and managing.

I would guess that the second explanation would be more valid. He simply was not self-aware that he was a poor manager, an unacceptably poor manager at that. We have all had bad bosses, bad managers and bad leaders. If we look back, we will realize that in most cases, it was not because they intentionally wanted to be bad bosses and managers. In most cases, it would be because they were simply not aware that they were lousy managers.

What I observed is that most people think they are good leaders and managers. In my fifty-two years, I am yet to meet someone who voluntarily says that they are a poor leader/manager/boss to their team. Everyone thinks that they are good or at the very least at an acceptable level as managers and leaders. Yet, we all know that the world is awash with bad managers and bad leaders. That is the paradox. Most bad managers and leaders don't start out with the intent to be bad—everyone wants to be good—but seldom do people have the self-awareness to know they are bad. And that problem might not be confined to just them. *You* and *I* could be a part of that list, a list of people who think they are good at people management but are actually lousy and lack the self-awareness.

The key to solving that problem is two-pronged:

1. Gain self-awareness
2. Set standards for yourself for further improvement

In this chapter, I am going to get you to do a set of exercises to help you gain awareness and set future standards for yourself. Let me repeat the earlier request—please do not skip any of the exercises in the book, they are important for your learning and awareness. Also please do these exercises with honesty and diligence, it will help.

Gaining self-awareness

Exercise 1: The 'ideal boss' visualization exercise

Visualize an ideal boss, the perfect manager whom you would like to report to. It does not have to be a real person you know; you can simply visualize a perfect manager.

Now list down all the expectations you would have from a perfect manager. For e.g., my expectations from a perfect manager would be a person who would:

- help me learn and coach me
- help me grow in my career
- not shout or insult me in public
- be generous in praising me when I do a good job
- be good at sharing credit when it is due

I have many expectations from a perfect manager. The list might be at least twenty items long, but I have just listed five here as an example.

Write down your expectations from your perfect boss/manager in the list below. The list is purposefully numbered to twenty. If you have a list less than fifteen, you have possibly not applied yourself diligently to this exercise.

My expectations from a perfect manager

1.
2.
3.
4.
5.
6.
7.
8.
9.
10.
11.
12.
13.
14.
15.
16.
17.
18.
19.
20.

As you can see, most of us have high expectations from our managers and that is natural. Our boss/manager has a very high impact on us on a daily basis and we want that impact to be as positive and as beneficial for us as possible. Hence, it is but natural that we have many and high expectations, and there is nothing wrong with it.

Now, let us turn this around and see life from the point of view of you as a manager/boss. Most of us have a set of people who are reporting to us—it can be one person or it can be a large team, that does not matter. Sometimes these people can even be off rolls and not be company employees but are effectively reporting to you. Think of all the people reporting to you.

Now go back to the list you made and, for each of the expectations you have from your manager, assess yourself on how much of that you are doing for your team. If your team—the people reporting to you—would have those same expectations from you that you have from your manager, then how effectively would you measure up against them? Do this by rating yourself against each item on the list. Rate yourself on a scale of 1–5. If you think you meet that expectation perfectly then rate yourself 5; if you think you don't meet that expectation at all, then rate yourself 1 and, if you think you meet that expectation partially, then rate yourself somewhere between 2 and 4. Do this for each item on the list one by one, and please do it with adequate reflection and honesty.

Once you have completed the exercise, add up the total score of all the items on that list and then divide it by the number of items to arrive at an average rating per item. This is your current standard, your baseline; it could be 2.8 or 3.7 or 4.3. And your focus from now on is to try and improve this.

Hopefully, this exercise has started the process of self-awareness about how you are as a leader and a manager currently. In the workshops I conduct, I make people do this exercise and without exception, one thing emerges. *Our expectations from our managers are much greater than what we are currently doing as managers for our team.* We want our managers to treat us in a certain way; we want to be coached in difficult situations with patience; and we want help in our career growth, but we are currently not actively practising all those in our roles as managers for our teams.

I wrote the title of this chapter as '*Self-Awareness, Setting Standards and Authentic Leadership*'. I was actually tempted to title the chapter as '*Self-Awareness, Double Standards and Authentic Leadership*', but I resisted because I felt the words 'double standards' would be too harsh, aggressive and also undermine the self-awareness that I wanted you to eventually obtain through the exercises. In most cases, though, that is the hard truth. We do tend to have double standards. My expectations from my boss are much higher than what I am willing to do for my team and I am guessing that is true for most of you as well. I tip my hat to the few of you who are not like that—you will be in the company of a super minuscule minority. However, before you start celebrating, I would request you to reassess if you indeed did the exercise with adequate honesty and deep reflection.

If I were to give you a direct approach, the most effective way to becoming a great manager and leader would be to '*start doing for your team what you expect from your manager and your leader, irrespective of whether your manager/*

leader is meeting your expectations or not'. If you simply start doing this—identify those items on the list where your rating is the lowest and improve on them—you will start becoming a better manager and leader. And who knows, one day, you might be taking your manager's place because you have become much better at people management.

The issue of lack of self-awareness also seems to be a perpetual one—a bad manager remains a bad manager for a long time. They sometimes survive for decades being bad managers. A combination of producing results and companies being tolerant sustains this phenomenon of bad managers and leaders having longer lives than they should and accentuates the self-awareness problem. They think, 'I have survived this long being like this. That means I must be a good manager and there is no need for me to change anything' and so the saga continues. At this very moment, it is likely that most of us are visualizing bad managers from our past who we know to be like this. But we are still not considering the possibility that someone else may be visualizing *us—you* and *me*—like that.

The simplest way of assessing your current level as a manager is to see the average rating score at the end of the exercise. As a thumb rule I would say

Average Rating Manager classification

< 2	Terrible manager
2-3	Poor manager
3-4	Acceptable manager
4-5	Great manager

Of course, the above is based on the assumption that you did the exercise with diligence and honesty. If you did not do so, I would encourage you to do it again, although it would be less effective now since you know how it is used. Nevertheless, if you feel you did not do the exercise well, do repeat it. If you are honest with yourself at this point, which may also be based on feedback you may have received from your team at different points, it will yield you great dividends in the future as a great manager.

Setting standards for improvement

The above exercise also allows us to set standards for improvement. Most of us don't really have a clear goal on how to improve as managers/leaders. We just continue being managers and leaders on a daily basis and assume that we are improving. The above exercise does two things:

1. Where the rating is low to medium, it creates an urgency and motivation to improve which we otherwise lack.
2. It also gives us a broad set of areas to improve on, typically those in which we have very high expectations when it comes to our bosses, but ones that we are hardly practising for the team we are leading/managing.

An important thing to understand is that improvement is not only for those with low ratings but for everyone. Our expectations from our bosses, in a way, represent

our potential as leaders and managers. Till we reach a
rating of 5; till we start practising each of those perfectly
for our teams, there is an opportunity to improve.
Hence, even someone with a rating above 4 must aim
to get to 5. The reason I say so is because of the power
and impact of people management in making you
successful. In the introduction, we discussed four levers
which drive success—getting better continuously, career
management, life management and people management.
From those, people management is a lever which has a
very high impact. Even people who may not be highly
educated or may not possess the IQ of a genius, can still
get very far and become successful if they are superb at
people management. How good you can be at people
management does not have an upper limit—it is infinite.
It is only a function of what standard you set for yourself
and how aggressive you are in driving the improvement
strategy. Set a high standard, reach for the moon and leave
a legacy of being one of the most effective and loved.

Authenticity

Anyone who has even read a few books on leadership
would have come across this word 'authenticity' and
would have heard things like how important it is for a
leader to be authentic and how authentic leadership
is the way to go. Without disagreeing with the core
concept, I find that this is one of those fancy, done-to-
death words that get thrown around loosely anywhere
and everywhere. Additionally, it is neither well-defined
nor well-understood. When someone says that a person is

not an authentic leader and you probe further, you realize that they mean that the leader is not showing the honesty/ integrity required. If so, then why not say that the person is a leader who lacks integrity? Why would that person be an inauthentic leader? Sometimes when someone gets referred to as being highly authentic, you find that it is because they are fair and transparent and do not play favourites. If that is the case, it would be better to call them fair/transparent leaders, and not be confused with being 'authentic'.

Largely, there is a tendency to use the term 'authentic leader' in a general way to denote a good leader and it is often used as a catchphrase. That does injustice to the term. The concept of authentic leadership and authentic people management is a very powerful one if we truly understand and practise it.

Here is the way I like to think about it. You are authentic when the type of people management you practise is very closely aligned to the type of human being you are; the type of personality you are. It is very closely aligned to who you are. Authenticity is about being true to yourself. All of us do not have to be similar as people managers. We need to understand who we are as people, and evolve our own style of leadership. Let me explain with an example here.

I have had two extraordinary leaders who have led me in my corporate career—Bharat Puri and Anand Kripalu. Both were outstanding people managers; among the best you could get. But both were very different in their styles as people managers. Despite being different, they were very effective because their styles were aligned to who they were as human beings. They were authentic to who they were.

Bharat's style has been entrepreneurial. He was very happy to keep many different balls in the air at the same time. He was perfectly comfortable juggling many different initiatives at the same time. Anand, in some ways, was quite the opposite. Anand's mantra was that 'a few big things' will make a difference. 'Focus, focus, focus' was Anand's other catchphrase. Bharat depended a lot more on instinct and would back an initiative even if research showed it was risky. Anand believed in market research and would go with the results setting aside his gut.

Both Bharat and Anand were similar in their styles in one area—one never had to second guess where one stood with them on any issue. Whether they were in agreement or if they disagreed, it would be clear. Another point of similarity was their genuine concern for people. They would always have time for any employee who wanted to discuss a concern. A one-on-one meeting with either would never be interrupted with a phone call and one would have their full attention.

So, as you can see, both have been great managers, authentic to their own distinct personas. And it is this evolution—as leaders true to who they are as people—that makes them truly authentic leaders.

The best way to becoming a good manager is to become an authentic leader and manager, to build our leadership and managerial ethos based on the kind of humans we are; the kind of personalities we are and what is core to us. It is definitely not simple.

The next question which presents itself is—how does one find out what is authentic to us? In my developmental workshops, when I do the exercise of visualizing the ideal manager, I often get participants to read out some of their expectations from the lists they make. Here is the interesting thing—most people often have different expectations from an ideal manager and these are not common. And those expectations are different because they are different humans and personalities. This is absolutely okay. As you define your expectations from an ideal manager, don't try to follow anything another person may want, or any expectations you may have read about leaders—mention what is important to YOU.

Once you have made this list as defined in the exercise, it becomes a great starting point for identifying your own authentic leadership plan/path. Now pick out the expectations from this list that are most important to you—the critical ones. They will be closely aligned to your specific needs as an individual, linked to who you are. Now start practising them with your own team, the one you lead. These will be your authenticity spikes, and will help you become an authentic leader. Because you will be applying in practice your own deepest needs as a person—and evolving as the best manager you can become. Lead from your core.

Hopefully, this chapter has opened your mind to the need for self-awareness. To the fact that just continuing to be the leaders and managers we are on a daily basis is not going to make us better and that we might actually be poor or moderate leaders/managers without even knowing it. The rest of the book is going to give you tools and techniques to grow your ability to lead and manage, but awareness of the need to do so and the hunger to improve has to come from within.

Chapter summary:

1. Most people who are poor managers and leaders are not so because they intentionally want to be poor managers. It is just that they lack the self-awareness to know the truth. You and I could be on that list as well.
2. A good starting point to gaining self-awareness is to do the 'ideal boss' visualization exercise with all honesty and diligence and then rate yourself as a manager based on that. That is your current baseline and you need to improve from there.
3. We do tend to have double standards—our expectations from our leaders and managers are typically much higher than what we are willing to do for those who report to us. The simplest shortcut to becoming a better leader and manager is to close this gap. Start doing for your team what you expect from your manager. You will immediately start becoming better as a people manager.
4. Set yourself a standard; a goal to improve, so that you can become the best at people management as far as possible. People management is a high-impact lever on overall success. Good people management can neutralize a lot of other potential weaknesses such as moderate education, lack of a high IQ, etc., in the career success journey.

5. Authentic leadership is about leading and managing based on the kind of human you are. You can identify your authenticity spikes from seeing what your most important expectations from your manager are in the ideal boss visualization exercise. Your most important expectations would be different from others. Identify them and start practising them yourself with your team. By doing so, you will set the base for yourself as an authentic people manager.

3

Leading and Managing—Towards What End?

Once, my HR head came to me and said he was going to set up a buddy system for our leaders and managers where we would pair them up and they would meet regularly to share experiences and learn from each other. You are probably aware of many such similar buddy systems in many companies. My response was, 'Nice idea, but what problem are you trying to solve?' This led to the realization that the problem itself was unclear. We were trying to get clarity about the problem and arriving at an entirely different solution for it.

As I mentioned in the introduction chapter, there is too much focus on what we do in leading and managing and not enough on what impact it creates and what outcomes we want. Leaders and managers tend to focus on visibly showcasing their ability to act. So suddenly, someone will start 'coffee with X'; someone else will start Friday beers, someone will start regular one-on-ones and so on and so forth. Many of these are fashionable ideas and when leaders and managers start doing some of these, they begin to think that they are doing a better job of leading and managing. I personally have nothing against these ideas. In fact, I have even practised some of these, but the problem is when it is done mindlessly as an idea without knowing why it is being done. If you are unable to articulate what impact and what outcomes this will create for you as a leader and manager, then you might as well drink your coffee alone.

The same thing happens at companies' L&D department level in HR functions. The focus is on ideas without problem identification. Ideas like 360-degree feedback and coaching; leadership development workshops, etc., abound in all companies. Sometimes I wonder if all companies roughly do the same thing for leadership development, albeit with different names and packaging. Then they must all be having the same problems as well. Does that seem right?

The reason this 'one-size-fits-all' approach is prevalent is because there is inadequate focus on the impact and the outcomes required from the acts of leading and managing. It is imperative to ask—towards what end? That question is often not well-answered at both the individual and company levels. In this chapter, we shall try and understand the outcomes expected from us as leaders and managers. There is no point trying to improve on tools and techniques as leaders and managers without knowing what outcomes we want to improve on.

When it comes to determining the outcomes we want, there is another question that we need to answer— for whom do we want those outcomes? I like to use the word *stakeholder* to define the 'for whom'. For e.g., if I am a manager and I am working towards improving the performance of my team members, then in this case, the stakeholder is my team and the outcome to be improved is their performance. So even before we get to outcomes, it is important to understand who the stakeholders are. Once we identify the stakeholders, then we can define the outcomes for each of them separately.

Exercise: The Case of Goblin Ltd

I am going to give you a small case to help you understand the concept of stakeholders and the outcomes for each stakeholder. Once again, I will request you not to skip this exercise and work on it with diligence and adequate reflection. Read the case well and reflect on the two questions that I have subsequently raised. Write your answers in the space provided.

Goblin Ltd:

This case describes a hypothetical situation as of January 2022 in Goblin Ltd.

Dinesh was an important person in the sales team at Goblin Ltd. He had been performing effectively and had earned the reputation of a performer, someone who delivers on the numbers. He had been in this role for two years now and knew that if he delivered on his targets in 2022, then he would get an important promotion. He was determined, come what may, to deliver and get the incentive/ bonus for the year and that promotion he had been working towards. However, the economy was weak and this made his task more challenging, a challenge he transferred to his team as well.

Dinesh's key team members were Krishnan and Gauri. Krishnan was seen as a good resource and had the potential to rise very high in the organization if mentored well. However, of late, he was showing some signs of being less engaged. Gauri was a recent addition to the team, being one of the first women to be hired as a sales manager in Goblin as part of their effort to become more diverse. While she had positive intent, she was going through the challenges of settling in a new company and one that had very few women in sales.

Dinesh's boss, Azeem, was the national head of sales. He had been brought in from an established MNC with a focus on building systems and processes as historically Goblin Ltd had a very number-oriented culture with little focus on processes and systems.

Goblin's sales team had great relationships in the market and they primarily used those relationships to sell. They had minimal focus on analytics and scientific selling.

Robert, the HR head of Goblin, was in discussion with the MD of Goblin on the growing attrition in the sales team. They were worried about losing key talent and also the absence of a succession pipeline in the sales function. They were wondering how to solve that problem, especially since sales delivery was getting more and more challenging.

Q1. Put yourself in the shoes of Dinesh as on 31 December 2022. The year 2022 has passed. Dinesh is reflecting on the year gone by and one of the things he is thinking about is how effective he was as a leader and manager in 2022. What actions would Dinesh have had to take in 2022 for him to consider himself as an effective leader and manager? Please focus on the leader and manager part and not on business and strategy, technical aspects, financial aspects, etc. **Put yourself in Dinesh's shoes and write a list of the actions he took and the outcomes he achieved in his role for him to consider himself as a good leader and manager for 2022**. You are writing this from Dinesh's point of view. You have to imagine you are Dinesh when you do this. You are not an external person evaluating Dinesh nor are you someone from Goblin Ltd. You are Dinesh when you answer the question.

1.
2.
3.
4.
5.
6.
7.
8.
9.
10.

Q2. At the end of December 2022, Azeem, Robert and the MD meet to discuss Dinesh's performance as a leader and manager. Under what circumstances would they think that Dinesh did a good job of being a leader and manager for 2022? Again, the focus being on leader and manager and not financial or technical or business/strategy aspects, etc. Put yourself in their shoes and write down a list of what

Dinesh should have done for them to consider him a good leader and manager in 2022. For this exercise, you are Azeem, Robert and the MD.

1.
2.
3.
4.
5.
6.
7.
8.
9.
10.

Spend a few minutes and reflect on your learnings from this case and jot them down below before I share some of my insights.

Learning 1.

Learning 2.

Learning 3.

As I do this case in my workshops, here are how the group responses typically play out. To Q1 on when would Dinesh himself consider that he had done a good job as a leader and manager, the very basic answers that come from the group typically are:

1. I managed my team well to get them to perform in a manner that allowed me to meet my targets.
2. I helped them as their manager such that they also met their targets.

In a few cases, and the 'few' deserves emphasis, some higher order answers also emerge:

1. I helped Gauri settle down as a new employee and a woman manager into the sales system.
2. I understood Krishnan was a little anxious about his career and hence, he was getting disengaged. I spoke to the higher-ups and we made a career plan for Krishnan for the next few years which we shared with him. He is now less anxious and more committed to the job and Goblin.

The core learning for a lot of people, as the discussion progresses in the workshops, is that often, we as leaders and managers tend to think of stakeholders and outcomes in a very narrow way. Often, the primary stakeholder for us—as leaders and managers—is the self. We focus on how we can lead and manage our teams to ensure that we achieve our performance goals. Slightly more evolved leaders and managers also start thinking beyond their own performance to how they can lead and manage their teams to create positive performance outcomes for team members as well. Typically, that is where it stops. It takes a lot of prodding to getting to higher order answers like— making a contribution to company diversity by helping Gauri settle in or helping build careers for the team, etc.

The moment we start to look at this from the perspective of Azeem, Robert and the MD, things start to open up in our minds on what is expected of Dinesh as a leader and manager. In response to the question, 'What are the requirements from Dinesh for Azeem, Robert and the MD to consider that he had done a good job as a leader and manager for 2022?', a comprehensive list of answers would possibly look like this.

1. Dinesh did a good job of leading and managing his team to deliver the necessary business performance.
2. Despite the weak economy and high pressure of selling, Dinesh did a great job of balancing business delivery with his team's morale and engagement through his personal engagement and relationships with them.
3. Dinesh did a good job of reducing attrition in his team by identifying potential issues and solving them proactively where suitable. An example of this was how he managed Krishnan's career ambition.
4. Dinesh embraced the company objective of diversity and helped stabilize Gauri, one of the first woman managers in sales. In the bargain, he has developed processes for how to induct and stabilize more women managers in the future.
5. Dinesh embraced the shift from relationship-based selling to a more scientific and analytics-based approach. He has actively coached his team to be able to make this transition as well.
6. Dinesh identified and helped develop future talent for the sales succession pipeline by active coaching

and development of identified high potential talent.

I think you get the picture by now. If we think of ourselves as leaders and managers from just our own eyes, then we tend to have very narrow outcomes and objectives in our minds for what we need to achieve. But if we tend to think of ourselves as leaders and managers from the perspective of all stakeholders, then we are able to understand the more holistic set of outcomes expected from us. And that is what will make us great at leading and managing.

A possible list of stakeholders and the outcomes they would expect from you as a leader and manager could potentially look like this:

Stakeholders	Outcomes
My company and its leadership	Attracting and retaining good talent, building succession pipeline, driving company-wide change agendas, implementation of initiatives promoting diversity and culture.
My boss/manager	Enabling his performance and enabling implementation of his strategic objectives.
Me	My performance, my career, my learning

Stakeholders	Outcomes
My team	Their performance, their career, their learning and development. A place they enjoy working in.
People below my team	Vision and direction, motivation, indirect career support. Creating a good work environment.

I have not tried to be fully comprehensive as that would mean the creation of a long list. The purpose of the list above is to give you a flavour of how you think about stakeholders and outcomes as a leader and manager. Towards the end of this chapter, I will get you to draw this list for yourself to establish a current baseline.

This concept of stakeholders and outcomes is another yardstick to evaluate ourselves as to how good we are as leaders and managers.

1. The **worst** leaders and managers are those who focus only on one stakeholder—themselves. They lead and manage their teams to basically improve their own performance for their own career and growth purposes. We have all experienced working with such people who are so selfish in focusing on what's good for them that they really don't care about other stakeholders.
2. The **poor** leaders and managers are those who add one more stakeholder; either their team or their boss, but not both.

a. Those who add their boss/managers as the second stakeholder become a real pain for their teams. Such people, apart from managing their own performance and career, are very focused on upward management. In trying to meet every demand of their manager, they often drive their team crazy with impossible demands and constant changes.

b. The other kind of poor leader is one who adds their team as the second stakeholder but does not add the boss. Such people are very focused on meeting their team's demands without really giving equal importance to organizational objectives and the direction the boss is providing. They often are difficult to convince for difficult stretch targets and initiatives or for big, bold change agendas which could cause discomfort to their team. In some phases of my own career, I have been guilty of sitting here.

3. The **good** leaders and managers are those who, apart from including themselves as a stakeholder, take on both the other stakeholders—their team and their manager. By doing this, they are balancing conflict and varying demands, one of the most challenging things that one has to do as a leader. Such leaders are able to understand the needs of the manager and their strategic objectives and get them implemented through their teams. At the same time, they are able to understand the team's needs and aspirations and effectively represent that to the manager and try

and fulfil those as well. Continuously balancing all stakeholders effectively, without tilting too much to one side, while meeting their own performance and career needs is the mark of a good leader.

4. **Great** leaders and managers are those who recognize the need to engage with all stakeholders; keep an eye on all outcomes expected and are able to function as holistic leaders and managers. Apart from themselves and their immediate bosses and direct reports as stakeholders, they also recognize the company and its leadership as a stakeholder. They understand that in their role as leaders and managers, they have to be effective in attracting and retaining talent, drive change agendas, etc. They also recognize the organization below their direct team as a stakeholder and are able to provide them with the vision and motivation as well to support their career development.

This continuum also often represents the nature of the career progression path that we see people going through. Those who get stuck in their careers are often the worst and belong to the poor category. They make progress to some extent, but then get stuck fairly early in their careers. The 'good' category move ahead to a reasonable extent but most of them fall shy of senior management. It is the 'great' category that makes it to senior management, and more importantly, succeeds at senior management.

I have seen that in high volume, large employer base industries like IT, banking, etc., getting stuck in one's career after becoming a manager is particularly prevalent and that is often because they are not able to evolve from managing the outcomes of one or two stakeholders to becoming holistic leaders handling the expectations and outcomes of multiple stakeholders and multiple outcomes. This problem can't be solved after you become part of the senior management. You have to learn to lead and manage the full spectrum of stakeholders and outcomes even before you get to the 'leadership' position. One of my favourite sayings which I don't tire of repeating is, *'People who reach senior leadership positions are those who start to lead and manage like senior leaders even before they get to that position'*. Go ahead, lead and manage holistically towards delivering multiple outcomes for multiple stakeholders and you will see it positively impact your career.

A starting point to delivering to multiple stakeholders and outcomes is to be able to list them down uniquely for you. What I did earlier was a generic exercise. Before we enter the next part of the book, it is important for you to do a specific exercise to map your stakeholders and the outcomes they expect in a similar table as we did earlier. Here it is important that you be specific. Don't write 'my boss', instead write the person's name and the specific outcomes that person has from you as a leader and manager. This is not about all the KRAs but outcomes expected as a leader and manager. Similarly, write your team members' names and their expectations from you as their leader and manager. One person may need career support, another may need coaching for performance, etc. Write names and specific outcomes in the space below.

Stakeholders	Outcomes
My company and its leadership	
My boss/manager (write name)	
Me	
My team (write each person's name)	
People below my team	

It is very important to do this exercise now. As we progress through to the next sections of the book to understand various tools and techniques to lead and manage well, you will be able to correlate and select specific tools and techniques for the stakeholders and the outcomes that you need to deliver. At the end of this exercise, I want you to reflect and rate yourself on how many stakeholders you have been focusing on till now as a leader and manager. You can rate yourself between 1 and 5 based on the number of stakeholders whose outcomes you have been actively trying to deliver. It is a self-assessment and you can be honest to yourself.

This, so far, is from the individual point of view. If we look at it from the company perspective, a similar approach works. We need to look at problem identification and stakeholder identification first, before beginning to generate a number of ideas on how to solve for them. I will go back to my earlier question now that the L&D function needs to ask. At a company level, towards what end are we doing this? And as we saw for individuals, they then need to identify 'for whom do we want these outcomes?' That will then lead to defining stakeholders, and subsequently defining the outcomes they want for each stakeholder separately.

That, at a company level, will lead to a two-tiered approach.

1. Which are the teams/functions/groups we want to create outcomes for?
2. Specific programmes thereafter to solve specific problems, for each of these stakeholders. For example, if a company is facing severe attrition and performance problems because their managers are not leading and managing their teams well, then a specific programme is required for that. And that programme would be very different from another company where the problem they are solving is attracting, developing and retaining high-potential talent and how to develop leaders and managers capable of doing that.

Without this kind of focused thinking around stakeholders and outcomes, L&D functions may end up frittering their resources and energies away on many disparate programmes, simply because they worked for another company, or because they are popular, without much impact.

Chapter summary:

1. In our efforts to lead and manage, too much focus goes into what we want to do and too little on why

we want to do it—the outcomes we want. This is true both at individual and company levels.

2. To understand outcomes, we have to also understand who the stakeholders are to us as leaders and managers and the outcomes that each of the stakeholders expects from us.

3. There are potentially five stakeholders. The list starts with 'me', then one down and one up, i.e., my team and my boss and then two down and two up, i.e., the people below my direct team and my company and its leadership.

4. Each of these stakeholders has a different set of outcomes that they expect from us as leaders and managers and it is important to identify that in advance for you to be effective.

5. The worst leaders are those who manage for only one stakeholder—themselves. Poor leaders manage for two stakeholders, themselves and a second stakeholder, either one up or down. Good leaders take both one up and one down and manage outcomes for three stakeholders. Great leaders lead and manage for outcomes expected from all stakeholders.

Summary: Section 1 and introduction to Section 2

In the introduction, we began with the importance of being good at people management with respect to becoming successful. The means to becoming good at people management is to lead and manage. We agreed that it is not an either/or but an 'and'. Hence, each one of us has to do both. We also covered the fact that it is not important what we are called—our title—but our focus has to be on the action. Whether we are called a leader or a manager is less important than whether we are leading and managing.

We defined managing as the art of impacting people by being directly involved and leading as the art of impacting people without being directly involved. Understanding these definitions is important as they guide what we have to do to improve in leading and managing. The concept of universality is important; every person has an opportunity to both lead and manage and every situation has the opportunity to deliver both leading and managing outcomes.

A core building block to becoming a good leader and manager is self-awareness. Bad leaders and managers don't start out by saying they want to be bad; they are simply not self-aware. This self-awareness coupled with setting standards for the future and identifying your themes of authentic leadership can set a platform for you to grow further as a leader and manager.

In parallel, it is important to become aware of the outcomes that are expected of us as leaders and managers.

This requires us to become aware of the various stakeholders we impact and their outcome expectations. It is important not to be narrow and focus on just one or two stakeholders but to be holistic in our leadership and deliver multiple outcomes to multiple stakeholders.

If I were to summarize this comprehensively, this is what I would say:

> *People management is crucial to succeed in your career. Good people management requires you to be both a leader and a manager and not just one. It also requires you to focus on the action of leading and managing. Heightened self-awareness and high standards for the future ensure that you improve continuously. This continuous improvement can be targeted at meeting outcomes for all stakeholders.*

The next section of the book is about how to be good at managing and the section that follows will give you tools and techniques for leading. As you read those sections, I want you to continuously keep connecting to your reality. Use your heightened self-awareness to identify those areas which you need to improve in terms of being both a leader and a manager in an effective manner. Similarly, use your understanding of stakeholders and outcomes and then connect the concepts in the next two sections to potentially solve for those outcomes and stakeholders that you are not addressing today. Don't just read them as concepts.

A bit on the immediate next section on managing: As discussed, managing well is the foundation to being successful; it is difficult to succeed by being a bad manager.

You need to have a positive impact on the people you are directly involved with and most often, this is your own team. To manage your team well and to have a positive impact on them, you have to be able to do three things:

1. Manage their performance. Their performance must be better because you are their manager.
2. Manage the performer, the human being. Their mental and emotional needs, their career and development needs, etc.
3. Manage the team as opposed to individuals.

The next three chapters will cover these in detail. Happy reading and best wishes in the journey of transforming into a great manager!

SECTION 2

4

Managing the Performance

We have discussed the importance of being a good manager when it comes to harnessing the lever of people management. As the name of the lever suggests, managing people around us is a critical task. And with no one is it more important than with those people who directly report to us. To really be called a well-performing manager, we also need to manage the performance of our direct team. This performance can be measured in targets or KPIs or goal sheets—different companies use different terminologies—but getting your team to deliver the requisite performance is an important job for a manager. And as we concluded before, everyone is a leader and manager and hence this is not intended just for managers. Even a CEO has a set of people reporting directly to her and getting them to deliver is as key a task for the CEO as it is for a junior manager.

I was once observing a performance review meeting. As you are aware, most companies have periodic performance review meetings—they could be daily, weekly, monthly, etc. This was an HR performance review meeting. There was a discussion regarding the inadequacies in the talent acquisition process and hiring of new people. At the end of the meeting, it was agreed that to improve chances of hiring, instead of interviewing two candidates per vacant position, we were now going to interview four. As soon as the meeting got over, I saw the talent acquisition manager call one of her team members and say, 'From tomorrow, for every vacant position we must see four candidates.' I am not sure what the other person was saying, but from the tone I guessed that it was something about the fact that going from two to four in a few days was not feasible and there is a lot of groundwork involved, etc. But the manager was firm. This is the number one strategy used by managers when it comes to improving the performance of their teams, what I like to call 'make a mobile call'.

'Just make a call, ask your team member to improve the performance from tomorrow and the job is done.'

This strategy plays out in an even more interesting way in line functions like sales and production. After a typical sales performance review meeting, all the managers will troop out and each will find a corner to fish out their *performance improvement device*—the mobile phone—and start making calls.

Some calls will sound like this:

Manager: Ramesh, we have to improve sales performance. Our current weekly sales run rate is not enough.

Ramesh: But sir, the market is down and there is hardly any demand for our products.

Manager: Ramesh, this is not the time to worry about markets and all that. We will discuss those things when we meet for the annual review. Right now, you have to increase your weekly sales from ten units to fourteen units from next week onwards.

Ramesh: But sir, the ten units I sold last week itself are still with the distributor . . .

Manager: Ramesh, this is not the time for *if*s and *but*s. I have made a commitment to our GM that we will improve our sales performance. You are going to help keep the commitment of our team, aren't you?

Ramesh: Errrrr . . . yes sir.

Manager: That is the spirit, Ramesh. I always knew I could count on you. Remember . . . fourteen units.

While the call itself is funny, what is even funnier is that *the manager, at the end of the call, thinks that he has actually done something which will improve Ramesh's sales performance.* After all, the manager has made a phone call asking for improved performance. I sometimes think it is these mobile phone and telecom companies that somehow surreptitiously introduced the concept of performance review meetings in companies. The greater the number of performance review meetings, the greater is the number of calls that are made, the more voice and data units are consumed and eventually, more phones get sold.

I am quite convinced that most of us have used this strategy for improving the performance of our teams. Though I am poking fun at this strategy, it does work in a few circumstances. If we don't want to call it a 'make a mobile call strategy', then we could call it an 'ask for better performance' strategy, either on a call or on email or face-to-face. The 'ask for better performance' strategy works under very few circumstances, primarily when the team member has been slacking off, or deliberately not doing the needful, or if the manager has somehow not clearly asked for better performance.

But assuming that most of our team members are decent, hard-working, honest people, this strategy seldom works except in creating a false sense of satisfaction for the manager, '*I have taken some steps to get better performance from my team member*'.

And when this strategy fails to obtain the desired performance, then the next week's call is a little longer with a sterner tone of voice and mobile phone companies prepare to celebrate!

Why do even experienced managers often fall into the trap of the 'ask for better performance' strategy? It happens because many a time, managers don't have a good understanding of what variables actually impact performance in a structured way. Some people have some awareness of the variables—be they internal or external— affecting the team and organization, such as market scenarios, underperforming employees or even a lack of clear direction and oversight from senior managers.

But those often seem too time-consuming and hence 'ask for better performance' becomes a here-and-now easy shortcut.

I want to introduce a framework which will help you think about managing for performance in a holistic way. Before I get to the framework, I want to add a caveat. We are talking about the human and managerial aspects of driving performance. There are other things that impact performance like price of a product/service, economy, competition, quality of products and services, quality of available equipment, quality of software and analytics, and so on and so forth. Those are not in our purview. We are focused on how you, as a manager, can manage your direct team for performance through human and managerial drivers.

The PAMOD framework

A very simple framework to think about performance is called PAMOD, an acronym for the equation below.

Performance = **A**bility x **M**otivation x **O**pportunity x **D**irection

Let us understand each of these terms well in the context of managing performance of team members.

Performance here refers to the performance delivered by your team members whichever way it is measured.

Ability is the inherent capability of your team members for the role they are essaying in your team. The higher the skill set and capabilities of your team member that are directly applicable to their role and daily activities, the higher is the chance of better performance and vice versa. Someone who is outgoing, charismatic and convincing is more likely to perform better in sales roles than someone who is less outgoing.

Motivation is about the morale, energy and commitment brought to the job by team members. It manifests in drive or lack of it. The greater the motivation, the higher the intensity that the team member brings to the job which can positively impact performance. A lack of motivation in a member who may be highly able, can lead to poor performance.

Opportunity is about the inherent opportunity for delivering performance in the role that the team member is playing. It is the ability of the organization and the environment surrounding that employee to enable them to deliver good performance. A number of things drive opportunity:

1. **Role and attention:** One team member could be in a high-priority role that has a lot of resources and senior management attention as opposed to another team member who could be in a low-priority role with limited resources and attention. This could impact the performance opportunity for both.
2. **Clarity of agenda and priorities:** There are many aspects to a given role, and hence, there needs to be clear prioritization among these, and a clear definition of the agenda. Lack of clarity can often lead to poorer

performance, as someone may end up working a lot on aspects that are low priority and hence, not contribute as much to their overall performance in the bargain.

3. **Availability of resources:** Opportunity is also about the availability of resources, people, money, materials and any other tools and resources required to deliver performance. The absence of these means that the team member does not have the opportunity to deliver desired performance due to a lack of resources.

Direction is about the support provided by the manager. Direction is a simple English word which can be interpreted in many ways. In PAMOD, I use direction as the way for the manager to be able to solve problems and issues which the team members themselves are unable to solve. This could be either solving complex problems being faced while the team member is performing the role; or it could be solving for challenging cross-functional and organizational issues for which the team member needs the manager's intervention.

That is PAMOD and that is the framework that explains how performance happens. I want you to put the book down and think about what are the top two or three insights that come to your mind as you absorb PAMOD. Do write them down here:

1.

2.

3.

Insights from PAMOD

Here are the implications of PAMOD.

Role of the team member, the manager and the organization:

The first thing that emerges from the PAMOD framework is that performance is not just a function of what the team member does. Often, many of us have a unidimensional view that a team member's performance is primarily dependent on them only—if it is good performance, it is because of them and if it is bad performance, it is because of them. As we consider the PAMOD framework, we see that ability and motivation are largely driven by team members themselves, though we, as managers, still have a role to play here as well. Opportunity and direction, on the other hand, are largely driven by managers, albeit with team members playing some role in it as well. Managing is the art of impacting people while being directly involved and if we examine the role that a manager has to play with respect to each of the four levers of PAMOD, it would look like this:

Ability: Manager impacts ability in the long term through coaching and development.

Motivation: Manager impacts motivation by creating the ideal work environment and culture and also potential rewards and career prospects.

Opportunity: Manager impacts opportunity by the role they assign to team members, how they set the agenda and priorities and ensure resources are available.

Direction: Manager impacts direction by solving problems that team members can't solve themselves and by enabling organizational and cross-functional support when team members need it.

As we can see, there is a significant impact that a manager has on the performance of a team member and yet, we as managers often think it is primarily the team member who is responsible for their own performance. I do not want to downplay the role of the team member in driving their own performance; it is, of course, vital. But in a book where we focus on understanding managing and leading, it is important for me to make you realize that *a lot of the performance of your team is a result of what you do as a manager.*

An interesting way in which the manager's impact on a team's performance manifests itself in companies is how, suddenly, a group of team members in a certain plant/office/sales zone starts performing well. When you look closely, it is clear that there is a manager there in that plant/office/sales zone who is positively impacting the performance of every team member.

Once, I was part of a performance review in my time in Asian Paints, and I noticed that suddenly, all the sales managers of the north zone had started performing well. It was quite unusual because among the eight–ten managers, there was not even one who was underperforming—every single one of them was performing very well. And the answer was clear—the north zone had got a new zonal sales head, Amit Syngle. Syngle's impact on the performance of his team members was a tremendous positive. It is not by accident that Amit Syngle has had a glorious career in Asian Paints rising all the way to becoming the managing director.

If you look around your company, you will find many such examples of team members in a zone or factory or an office or a function suddenly doing well, and this is often because of the managers. As a manager, the key question you need to answer is, 'Can you, with confidence, say that you have positively impacted and improved your team members' performance?'

There is a saying that 'the rising tide lifts all boats'; I like to tweak it to say 'a good manager lifts every team member's performance'. Are you such a manager? Can you say with conviction that your team members are performing better because you are their manager? And if you were not their manager, would they possibly perform to a lesser extent with another?

Are you the rising tide for your team members?

Poor performance is not equal to a poor employee:

I was asking the production head at the head office why the production in unit number seven in the south had been so poor. Pat came the answer, 'The plant manager there is not good.' You would also have noticed this tendency of quickly attributing poor performance to a team member. It is like good performance means a good team member and bad performance means a bad team member. But what PAMOD tells us is that performance is a function of the AMOD. Multiple people influence that and hence, for us to jump to a quick conclusion about team members is inappropriate.

To conclude that it is indeed the team member that is the problem, we must first do a due diligence using PAMOD and satisfy ourselves that O and D are not problems. This requires tremendous honesty because when we acknowledge that O and D are indeed problems, we are pointing the finger at ourselves, the managers. Once we conclude that O and D are not problems, then we need to check for M. If the team member is not motivated, then we need to check for inherent reasons—this can be both due to the team member as well as other reasons. Other reasons could include shabby treatment by the manager, promotion and career issues, etc. Only once we rule out other issues can we conclude that there is possibly an inherent motivation issue. And the final piece to come to is ability—we need to check if the team member's ability is really the problem. Here again, we must make sure that we eliminate organizational factors; for e.g., an individual might have high ability in one area but might be a misfit in the current role. It is only when we ascertain that the core ability of the individual is the problem, possibly along with core motivation, can we conclude that poor performance is because of the individual. I would request all my readers— the managers out there—to change the 'shoot first' tactic of blaming poor performance on individuals immediately. *If we don't want our managers to do that to us, then we must also not do the same to our team.*

Short-term versus long-term impact:

If you look at the PAMOD framework to see the levers that affect performance, then it is quite obvious that some of the levers can be activated to improve short-term performance while others can only impact performance in the long term. If you want to influence your team members' performance, here and now, the two highest impact levers in the short term are O and D, and both levers are in the manager's hand.

As a manager, you can definitely impact opportunity by defining priorities within a role, as well as the agenda therein, which will help the team member perform better in the short run. Similarly, you can provide better direction in the short run by solving problems that the employee may have been unable to resolve on their own. These are simple ways of creating an immediate impact on performance as a manager.

Sometimes, motivation through incentives, etc. can also change short-term performance, but this is largely at operational/junior levels, and doesn't work at middle/top levels.

And lastly, ability cannot be changed in the short term, but if, as a manager, you can work at coaching and developing your team members, it can have a very high impact on their medium-/long-term performance.

Multiplicative model:

The last and key insight on the PAMOD model is that it is a multiplicative model.

Performance = Ability x Motivation x Opportunity x Direction

This means that any one thing increasing significantly can materially improve performance and vice versa. Any one thing worsening can negatively impact performance. The best way to think about performance is to keep all the four levers of AMOD reasonably effective. That will result in steady, effective performance. And a superb spike performance happens when all levers are effective and any of the levers is upped to multiply the effect. For e.g., all things remaining equal, if we are able to find a new opportunity/priority which can have high impact, then deploying ability, motivation and direction on that new opportunity can create a superior performance. And when performance crashes, it can often be just because of one of the levers. As managers, if we can identify that and fix it jointly with the team member, performance can bounce back up quickly.

Application of PAMOD

Now that we have understood the model, let us spend time on how to apply this model for improving the performance of team members reporting to us. PAMOD is a versatile model and can be used either diagnostically or for planning. Let us briefly discuss both applications.

Diagnosing the problems in the past:

As a manager, you can use PAMOD to diagnose any problems in the past performance of your team members and use that diagnosis to identify improvement and development areas. After that, discussions regarding why these weaknesses came to exist and what solutions can be implemented separately and jointly to drive performance can be conducted. This diagnosis can be for the past year or the past quarter or for a specific initiative—it is whatever area or time frame you choose to apply the framework on.

When diagnosing the past, one suggestion I would give is—do not look at the overall macro performance first and then look for which lever explains that performance. Instead, look lever by lever objectively, from the beginning. Let me give you some leading questions which you can think about in the context of the performance you are reviewing:

Ability:

1. Were there areas where other team members seemed to solve problems easily but this person found it difficult to? At the same time, was there evidence of the opposite? Were there areas where other team members needed your help as the manager to solve the problem but this person could independently manage without any help?
2. In case of common problems which affect all team members or a future planning situation for the whole team, does this person contribute effectively or is the contribution muted?
3. Is the person aware and on top of the key metrics relating to how their area of business is operating and

performing, the numbers and drivers of their role, or are they clueless, at times, on important metrics?

Motivation:

1. Was the person fully committed throughout or was there some ebb and flow?
2. Were there frequent unexplained absences, excuses for avoiding attending challenging and important meetings, or was it the opposite? Was the person raring to go to participate in important forums and tasks and make a contribution?
3. Was there a tendency to complain a lot and feel helpless or was the person, while highlighting problems, being positive and giving a positive sense of wanting to solve the problem?

Opportunity:

1. Did we identify the biggest opportunities for superior performance in the role and prioritize them or was it a series of random things against which effort and resources were consumed?
2. Were resources a constraint or were they available in adequate measure?
3. Were there uncontrollable external dynamics like economy, competitive factors or natural disasters which either positively or negatively impacted the opportunity for performance significantly for this individual more than for other team members?

Direction:

1. Were complex problems which were beyond the ability of the team member left festering or did the manager help solve them?
2. Were cross-functional challenges like availability of the correct IT solutions, logistics, HR issues, etc., resolved with the help of the manager or did these become barriers to performance?

I have only given you a starting point of leading questions to think about the diagnosis. You can add to your own list given your context, knowledge and experience and arrive at your point of view of the current status of AMOD of your team member(s) and hence, its impact on performance. I recommend that you use a scale of 1–5 with 1 being the lowest and 5 being the best. Let us say that after the diagnostic, if you rate someone 2 for ability, it means you think that person has moderate ability when compared to what is required for the role. In a similar manner, assign ratings for all of PAMOD based on your diagnostic. Once you complete the diagnosis for yourself, I advocate the following steps:

1. Ask your team member to do a self-diagnosis using the PAMOD framework.
2. Organize a meeting where you both discuss your respective diagnostics and arrive at a common diagnosis.
3. Based on the common diagnosis, make a plan to further improve performance in the future.

A couple of pointers here.

Firstly, diagnosis is not just to be applied in poor performance situations, it can also be applied to good performance situations. It is simply about what we can learn jointly from the performance in the past so that we can better it in the future.

Second, there is often a great reluctance amongst managers to have that joint meeting to discuss the diagnosis. There could be different reasons for it, but do understand that to manage the performance of your team member, you have to discuss the drivers of performance with them in an objective way. If all we do is ask for better performance through a mobile phone, it will not work. So, it is important for each one of us to overcome the diffidence and have that detailed objective meeting on the diagnostic. It could also feel uncomfortable if the team member cites poor direction as an issue, but that is good feedback. Either you agree and improve on it or you convince your team member that the direction provided is adequate.

Third, the purpose of the diagnostic exercise is to learn from the past so that the future can be even better; it is not intended to criticize the past as that creates defensiveness which results in non-productive effort. As a manager, you must keep in mind that it is important to create a holistic and open environment, for these kinds of discussions. Your team members must not perceive this exercise as some sort of negative evaluation of their performance which they think could impact the future opportunities and relationship with the manager. If they feel that way, it would likely bias the employees into not doing the exercise with truthful diligence.

Planning for the future

The other way PAMOD can be very effective is to use it to plan for future performance. It is very simple. If you want future performance to be better than past performance, then something in AMOD has to change for the better. If nothing in AMOD changes, then it is unlikely that performance will improve. So, you have to plan for what in AMOD needs to change and how you will make it change.

Planning for the future does require a PAMOD baseline of the past. This inherently means doing a diagnostic as a starting point. Once you have a baseline, you will have developed a structured opinion as to which element among AMOD, if changed, has the highest potential to drive future performance. You will be able to do this using the kind of leading questions we identified for the diagnosis of past performance. Then, you will have to ask your team member to do the same independently. Finally, you will need to discuss and agree on which element amongst AMOD shows the highest potential for driving future performance and make an action plan around that.

Again a few pointers.

1. First, having a target for the next year or the next initiative's performance can be a double-edged sword when doing this exercise. On the positive side, having

a target/KPI can allow us to understand how much change we have to drive in one of the AMOD elements to get to that target. If we do not set a performance improvement target, we might not drive adequate positive change through AMOD. But at the same time, having a target, at times, ends up converting the meeting to a target negotiation exercise rather than a PAMOD exercise. This is a call you have to take case by case as a manager.

2. Secondly, sometimes, there is a temptation to choose every element of AMOD for change, to try and improve each one of it. That often does not work. I find that the greatest change in performance happens when we are able to identify the ONE highest potential element out of AMOD and then drive change in it. In the worst-case scenario, sometimes you could have two. But going beyond that seldom works effectively.

PAMOD exercise:

I would now like you to practise application of PAMOD. I want you choose one team member of yours who has not been performing too well and one team member whose performance has been good. Now, for both of them, prepare a

1. PAMOD diagnosis
2. PAMOD plan for the next year

I am not leaving space here for this exercise. You can use your own sheets of paper for this, but that does not diminish the importance of this exercise. It is one through which you can start identifying improvement areas and drive increased performance right away.

PAMOD is one of the most powerful tools that you have as a manager to improve the performance of your team. And when you continuously improve the performance of your team, then your career is magically transformed. Your leaders notice you as someone who consistently gets teams to perform and that opens up tremendous opportunities for you to grow. At the same time, other people working in the organization start to notice that working with you could improve their performance and their career prospects and soon, the best in the company would want to be a part of your team. This creates a virtuous cycle where you attract the best; and your performance automatically improves, thus positively impacting your career.

As I said in the introduction, my observation of successful people has been that they are effective in people management. One of the most important things they do well is positively impact the performance of their teams, which transforms their own performance and creates great success for them. That is the opportunity you have. If you can confidently say that my team members' performance is better because I am their manager and they are less likely to perform just as well with another manager, then you are on your way to a superb career. And the magic key to be able to do that is called PAMOD.

Self-application of PAMOD

PAMOD is an interesting tool that you can use not just for your team's performance, but also your own. If you do an honest diagnosis; make a good plan to improve for the future and implement that plan, your performance will improve. I too have used it often as a diagnostic tool. Whenever I felt unhappy about my performance, I applied PAMOD and would arrive at the answers. Many a time, the answer was around opportunity. Usually, any role has infinite potential for delivering high performance. However, often I would find myself working on lower order priority items instead of really focusing my energies on the big things that mattered. Changing that would change my performance fairly quickly. The second challenge would often be motivation. There would be times when I was not giving my 100 per cent to the role, basically doing a passable job where no one could find fault, but I was not giving it all that I had. Again, this is something that creeps in slowly. It is not that one fine day you suddenly lose motivation. PAMOD often helped me understand when I was not at my best and gave me the energy to push back and get back to my best again. I would urge each one of you to also use PAMOD for your own performance. The key, as always, is being honest when you use it. Do not externalize your problems. Best wishes for a great performance!

Chapter summary:

1. As a manager, managing your team's performance is one of the most important tasks. Many of us fall into the trap of the 'make a mobile call' or what I call the 'ask for better performance' strategy which seldom works.
2. To manage performance, we need to understand the human and managerial drivers of performance (excluding business and technical aspects).
3. PAMOD is an ideal framework to understand human and managerial drivers.

Performance = **A**bility x **M**otivation x **O**pportunity x **D**irection.

4. Key insights from PAMOD include:

    a. Performance is not just a function of the performance of the team member, the manager too plays a great role.
    b. We must resist simplifying 'bad performance = bad team member' and carry out an objective assessment through PAMOD before we conclude that it was the team member alone who was the reason.
    c. Performance in the short term can be primarily improved by driving O and D while long-term performance can be hugely improved by enhancing the team member's ability through coaching.

d. It is a multiplicative model and hence, the best approach is to keep all four elements of AMOD at a good level.

5. Application of PAMOD can be from two angles:

   a. Diagnosis of the past to find improvement areas and making an action plan.
   b. As a planning tool to plan for superior future performance.

6. Most successful people I have observed became successful because they positively impacted their team's performance as managers. If you continuously impact your team's performance positively, career success is a natural conclusion.

7. PAMOD need not be used just for your team members. You can also use it to improve your own performance provided you bring honesty to the analysis and do not externalize the problems you identify.

5

Managing the Performer

One of the most important things I advocate to all managers is to separate the *performance* from the *performer*. The performance your team member delivered is the output they gave. The performer is the human being behind that—the person in flesh and blood—with a brain, a heart, emotions and feelings, and aspirations and worries. There are two common mistakes managers make in this context. First, just managing for performance and not managing the performer is among the most common mistakes I see many managers make—one that I too have made in my early years. It took me many years to figure out that performance and performer are two different things and I have to manage both separately. The second mistake is the interchangeable and loose usage of both words. Testimony to that are casual comments like, 'Sheetal is a poor performer, she did a bad job of the project I gave her last quarter.' If Sheetal did a poor job of the project, then the more accurate statement should be,

'Sheetal demonstrated poor **performance** in the project I gave her last quarter.' It cannot be, 'Sheetal is a poor **performer**.' Separating the performance from the performer and not using these words interchangeably is important.

Focusing too much on performance and focusing less on the performer is a mistake made not just by managers but even by companies. Here is an anecdote from my experience. I had just joined a new company and there was an annual awards function which I got to attend. I saw that one particular individual was feted many times that night and everyone was singing his praises. After the formal event was over, I walked up to that person, introduced myself and congratulated him saying, 'Wow, you must be a very highly valued person in this company.' He was a seasoned veteran and replied, 'They are not celebrating me. They are celebrating my performance for last year. Next year, if I don't perform, I will be somewhere in the back, clapping for someone else's performance. And the people who sang my praises today may not even have the time to say hello.' Then he said something, which for me, was the clincher and has stayed with me till date. *'The day they **celebrate me and not my performance** is the day I will feel valued in this company.'*

The worst manifestation of this is the often bandied about expression—'You are as good as your last quarter.' And when such things are said in a group setting, people often laugh it off. But, in reality, such statements—where we reduce human beings to a transaction—are very damaging. I am not on a mission to change companies. The smarter ones are already changing and realizing that you can't hold on to talent with this short-sighted approach. But I am on a mission to change you—manager by manager—so that put together, we can create two benefits:

1. Make the corporate and entrepreneurial world a better place for each one of us to work.
2. Make you a superb manager. Convert you **from a performance manager to a talent manager**, an important step in a successful career.

As managers, we are expected to attract and retain talent; create a succession pipeline; and create a great culture and work environment. These outcomes can only be met by managing the person, the performer. We need to transition from being 'a performance manager to a talent manager'. Being a talent manager means we are **holistically managing our team members both for performance and as performers**.

When we say, 'manage the performer', what factors of the performer are we talking about beyond just their performance? There are three broad areas:

1. *The human being.* Each member of our team is unique and displays different emotions, feelings and motivations. If we are able to manage them well for the kind of person they are—using different styles where required—then we will be able to bring out the best in them as opposed to managing everyone in a similar way. Don't underestimate this. A team member who truly believes that you care for them

and truly understand them will give you their absolute best. They will give you their 110 per cent each time.

2. *Their learning and development.* Helping team members develop themselves; acquire skills and capabilities, giving them opportunities to test and challenge themselves, are all vital for a manager. Your company also expects this since only when you develop your team members can you create a better talent pool for your company.

3. *Their career and rewards.* Helping them achieve a career commensurate to their potential and ensuring that they are rewarded fairly is crucial.

We will not spend too much time on rewards and incentives here as that is a combination of the manager's perspective and company policies. But we shall focus more on the areas that you as a manager can directly influence.

Does having to 'manage the performer' mean that we actually need to customize our approach for every single person in the team? While that is ideal and desirable, managers may not have the skills or the bandwidth to be able to do that. To effectively and practically do this, we can instead group people with similar characteristics together.

To facilitate this, let us consider the Ability-Motivation matrix (as shown below) which allows managers to group team members into four broad groups. These are the same terms that we discussed in the PAMOD framework: Ability and Motivation. In a way, we are picking those elements that are more inherent to the team member—the performer—to understand how best to leverage that person.

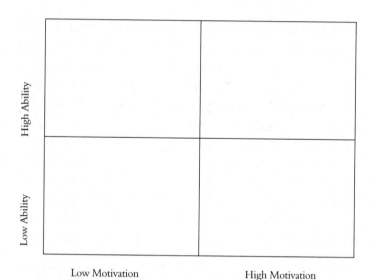

The vertical axis has Ability, split into high ability (HA) and low ability (LA), and the horizontal axis has Motivation, split into low motivation (LM) and high motivation (HM). This results in four different quadrants. The immediate visual understanding you can gain from the matrix is that you want your team members to be moving towards the top right quadrant.

One of my major observations has been that highly successful managers have most of their team members in the right half of the matrix, while less successful managers have more members in the left half. To become a successful manager, we have established that you need to move from being a 'performance manager' to a 'talent manager'. To enable this, your goal should be to help your team members move to that top right quadrant.

Depending on which quadrant each of your team members lies in, you can tailor your approach to manage them as a performer. We will go through each quadrant and try and understand the same in detail. I want you to take a quick minute and map key members of your team to this matrix in your mind. A quick effort will do for now; we will do a detailed one later. Keep the names of your team members in mind and the quadrant they belong to as we go through each. The exercise will be more relatable and effective this way.

Low Ability-High Motivation (LA-HM) quadrant
(bottom right quadrant)
(Think of one or two persons from your team who might be in this quadrant before you read the content)

This is typically where a new employee joins the company or an existing employee takes up a new role. They are high on motivation but relatively low on ability in the context of the role they have stepped into.

Team member situation:
In this quadrant, team members are typically very keen and eager to make a difference. They tend to ask a lot of questions and have a new way of looking at things. However, they also need a lot of help as they might not know the complexities of the role.

Role of the manager:
The manager must aim to help the person move up from LA to HA and eventually to the HA-HM quadrant.

An HA-HM team member is a great asset to the team and the manager. If the manager fails to do this, then eventually, the team member may move to the left of the grid and end up becoming an LA-LM person.

Approach of the manager:
In this situation, the manager must use a style which is a combination of coaching, direction and structure.

- *Coaching* is required to teach the person what is required for the role and make them capable of handling it independently over time.
- *Direction,* as we discussed, is solving those problems that the team members can't solve themselves. This is crucial in this quadrant—you can't leave the team member to solve really difficult problems, you must step in and help. Failure to do so can result in loss of confidence. Additionally, they need help with navigation within the organization and cross-functional issues that they would not be familiar with.
- *Structure* is important at this stage and requires setting a clear agenda and tasks with active reviews for the team member, otherwise they could get lost in a number of mostly irrelevant things.

People who are new to the role also bring in new ideas. So, while their ability with respect to the role might be low, it does not mean they cannot contribute at all. Openness from the manager to listen to their ideas and building on them together is another key requirement in this quadrant.

I made a big mistake once with a new team member who was in this quadrant. I made the error of not changing my approach towards this person from the one that I had towards the previous performer. The previous performer had spent considerable time with me, and that allowed me to operate with minimum supervision. When the new team member took on the role, by sheer habit, I continued my previous managerial style to very bad consequences. It took me three months to realize this and then, I corrected my approach to salvage the situation. But my mistake definitely damaged the confidence of the new person and I had to work on it over time to retrieve it. This is a very important mistake to guard against. Conscious effort must be made to change your approach towards a new person.

High Ability-Low Motivation quadrant (HA-LM) (top left quadrant)
(Think of one or two persons from your team who might be in this quadrant before you read the content)

Team member situation:
In this quadrant, team members are competent and possibly doing the job but they are emotionally flat—they are not bringing passion to the role or giving their best. They are possibly just going through the motions efficiently. Sometimes, team members in this quadrant can also be negative and cynical.

Role of the manager:
The first job of the manager here is to understand why they are low on motivation. There could be a couple of reasons:

a. They are high on ability for the current role, but not seen as someone who has the ability for future roles. As a result, they are not getting promoted. They have possibly been doing the same job for many years which has reduced their motivation and enthusiasm.

b. There could be working environment issues, poor relationships with managers/colleagues, etc. which has impacted their motivation.

The key, as a manager, in this situation is to have an honest analysis to arrive at the reason for the team member's low motivation including your own role in creating that.

Approach of the manager:
The approach of the manager here varies based on the reason for the low motivation. The first case we mentioned is a challenging one. Career progression, one of the key things which keeps people motivated in their career, has gone missing. The approach here should be to find alternate ways of motivating the person. Some ideas to consider would be to elevate the importance of the person even in the current role by allowing them freedom and responsibilities since they have the ability. One could also consider leveraging that person more extensively to represent you as the manager in various company forums and meetings.

I once saw a situation like this where the manager allowed the team member to make a full presentation to the senior management which they would have normally done. I noticed that the impact of that on the motivation of the team member was quite high, it gave that person a sense of pride and achievement. The manager can also adopt style factors like praise in public, listen to ideas and facilitate them, etc., to further keep them motivated.

Unfortunately, sometimes, in these situations, the individuals also become cynical and negative. They become power centres because they have spent a long time in the job and also speak negatively about the company. As a manager, you should not tolerate this. This is a slow spread of poison within the team. So, while on one hand, you may want to try and be positive and help them with alternate sources of motivation, on the other, deal with negativity strongly and clearly. An honest conversation with a clear communication that this is not acceptable is the starting point. If things don't improve even with that, then involve your HR team and take suitable steps. Don't let it fester.

The second case of low motivation could simply be poor relationship management and bad handling by you as the manager. We have all experienced low motivation when we are handled badly by our managers. Why could the same thing not happen to one of our team members? The starting point here is honesty and acceptance in our own mind that we might be part of the problem. Once we do that, then the next step is a good, honest, open conversation where you both agree on how you are going to try and improve the relationship, with both taking genuine steps.

High Ability-High Motivation (HA-HM) (upper right quadrant)
(Think of one or two persons from your team who might be in this quadrant before you read the content)

This is a quadrant of great opportunity but it takes a lot of skill as a manager to handle team members in this quadrant.

Team member situation:
Typically, people in this quadrant would have spent some time in the role and the company and would be very well settled. They are likely to be capable of solving complex problems, being independent and often contributing well beyond their role. They are also normally aware that they are very good and have expectations about their career which also need to be managed well.

Role of the manager:
The manager has two important roles here—one is to leverage the current high ability and motivation for creating high impact and the second is to facilitate their career progression.

Approach of the manager:
To leverage employees in this quadrant for high impact, it is important to give them the best of opportunities in high priority areas, and a chance to contribute beyond their role so that they stay charged and provide the best output. Sometimes, managers have an HA-HM team member, but they are not often given the most important things

to do. In a simple way, maximize the 'O' of PAMOD for such team members, the rest—A, M and D—are already in place. Managers should also delegate to such team members in a significant way so that they can operate independently.

It is also important to facilitate career progress for such team members. Managers need to keep an eye out for opportunities and at the right time, enable a new role for such team members. One of the challenges to this is the tendency of managers to hang on to such people because they are so effective. *They don't want to let them go.* That creates a negative cycle of frustration and eventually, the team member leaves the company for a career elsewhere, which is not a desirable outcome. Managers must overcome the reluctance to let go of good people to other roles within the same company which will create a positive cycle over time. Once, I let go of a star from my team without even having a person to replace them— which took 8 months—because I genuinely believe that it is not right for us to hinder a team member's career for our selfish reasons.

Occasionally, such team members also show the negative trait of acting like stars and prima donnas. Again, this is something you must deal with as a manager and not allow to fester, as it sets a very bad example for other members in your team. As always, an honest conversation is the starting point. Acknowledge their capabilities while also pointing out some of the undesirable behaviours. Go into it like a conversation, not a battle—you don't have to confront them, just talk to them. If this is done early enough from the time the problem has started, it will work.

Low Ability-Low Motivation (LA-LM) (lower left quadrant)
(Think of one or two persons from your team who might be in this quadrant before you read the content)

This is the most challenging quadrant and extracting a team member from here can be difficult, but not impossible. If and when you work hard and extricate a team member out of this phase, you will experience a great sense of satisfaction.

Team member situation:
Team members in this quadrant are often quite demoralized and seldom speak unless spoken to. They feel pressured; not in control and lack the confidence to do any important work without support. They also sometimes give the impression of being indifferent and not really bothered about work.

Approach of the manager:
The single biggest question to solve for here is why did the team member get to that quadrant? **No one starts there by intent**. We don't get into a job and say, 'I want to be low on motivation and ability in this job.' We always start in some other quadrant. So, in all probability, the team member has moved to this quadrant due to some pertinent reasons. These reasons are very important to try and understand because:

1. Once we understand the reasons, we can try and find solutions based on that.
2. Often, understanding the reasons motivates us to give our best shot at helping them.

Normally, as a manager, when we see such a team member, we almost always assume that the problem is with the team member. However, often, when we try to understand the history and problems, we find that the team member alone is not responsible for getting to this quadrant—it is a combination of current and past managerial actions, and organizational actions too may have contributed to this situation.

There are two quadrants you can attempt to move this person to. You can either try and move this person upwards to the HA-LM quadrant or towards the right to the LA-HM quadrant. In my judgement, trying to move someone who is currently low on motivation and low on ability to the HA-LM quadrant is very challenging. That is because it is very difficult to improve the ability of a team member when they are not motivated. Hence, I recommend that we must first attempt to move the team member to the LA-HM quadrant.

That means the first problem you must try and solve with the team member here is for motivation. And the magic phrase to that is, again, 'honest conversation'. This conversation will, however, require fair preparation, empathy and listening. The first step in the conversation is the acceptance of the problem by both parties in a non-judgemental way. The team member needs to accept the current situation and must also be able to see that the manager is not judgemental about it. The greater the lack of acceptance, the greater is the delay in solving the problem.

The next step in the conversation is getting a commitment from the team member that they are willing to fight to change the situation, motivate themselves, and find the discipline and energy to give it their best. There is a much higher chance of getting this commitment when the team member realizes that the manager is on their side and not against them or being a judge.

Once you gain the team member's acceptance and commitment to fight, it is very important to make sure that you also communicate the necessary commitment. If you continue like you did earlier, the team member's willingness to fight will fizzle out soon. You will have to commit greater energy and focus to that team member for a few months. Among the most important techniques I have used in this stage is to plan for small wins. Give them tasks which are relatively easy; support them when they do these and publicly acknowledge their wins when they get done. These small wins create a cycle of confidence and self-esteem which is very important for the team member to continue on a positive journey. Sometimes, this is where people make mistakes. After the honest conversation, and getting motivated to change, people tend to get overenthusiastic and often take up tasks aiming for the moon. If they fail at that, it becomes a big setback. Start with small wins and build gradually. The other key thing is to keep an eye on what is happening and step in to support as soon as you see the team member struggling. Help them out actively, sometimes even if it means doing the activity while sitting with them.

A few managers tend to think, 'This is too much hard work, and what's in it for me? Let me just get rid of this person and get a new person.' That is where the human aspect of being a manager comes in. As good humans, there are things we must do at times, not because there is a return in it for us, but because it is good for another human. And trust me, when you do it, you will get a return that won't be economic; it won't even have career benefits, but that return would be love, respect and your own satisfaction at having done something good.

Having said that, there are times when some people remain challenging and cannot be moved out of that quadrant despite your best efforts. When that happens, a different set of actions needs to be taken. I have written in detail about that later in this chapter. However, let us now complete our learning of the Ability-Motivation matrix before we go there.

Summary of the Ability-Motivation Matrix

HIGH	**Team member's situation**: Competent, lacking passion, just doing enough, sometimes negative and cynical. **Manager's role**: Needs to understand source of low motivation (career stagnation or work environment issues) and solve for that. **Approach of the manager**: In career stagnation, provide alternate motivation through exposure, responsibilities and empowerment. In work environment, first do a self-analysis of your role as a manager and then an honest two-way conversation to solve for any issues there.	**Team member's situation**: Has spent time in company and role, independent, produces results, contributes beyond the boundaries of the role, has career and growth expectations. Occasional 'star' behaviours. **Manager's role**: Leverage current high ability for impact and facilitate career progress. **Approach of the manager**: Provide high priority opportunities to work on challenging assignments and opportunities to contribute beyond the role. Empower. Facilitate career progress through active dialogue within the company and with the team member. Don't hang on, let them fly.
LOW	**Team member's situation**: Lacks confidence, demoralized, quiet and can be indifferent. **Manager's role**: Nobody starts here. Manager's role is to find out from where this person came here and why, to be able to find a solution. Change motivation and move them towards the right. **Approach of the manager**: Honest conversation to get two-way acceptance and the commitment of the team member to fight and change. Enable early small wins and celebrate them. Give active direction and support and don't let them fail at any task.	**Team member's situation**: New to company or role, keen and enthusiastic, asks questions, has new ideas, can't solve complex problems or cross-functional issues. **Manager's role**: Help move up to the high ability-high motivation (HA-HM) quadrant. **Approach of the manager**: Coach them to improve ability for the role. Provide them with direction and active support to solve complex issues. Set a clear agenda and task list.

Ability (vertical axis, left side)

LOW ←———————————————→ HIGH
Motivation

I hope this framework has given you a very actionable way of handling the performer, the human that is each one of your team members. Now, all the above is theory and when theory is not implemented, then it is not even worth the paper it is written on. It is therefore time to convert theory to practice. Connect this framework to your current reality and start to apply it; over time, you will become a master at it. What follows is one of the most crucial exercises of the book for you to apply and learn from.

Exercise

This exercise has four steps, two of which you will do now and the other two will need to be done on the field—in the real world—with your team. As always, honesty and reflection are the two hands to doing any exercise.

Step 1: Plot the position of your current team members in the matrix. Think deeply and objectively about it and don't be guided by any recent events. Take a slightly medium-term point of view.

Step 2: Write down the three key things for each team member—the team member's situation, the manager's role (your role) and the manager's approach (your approach). The important thing here is to be specific and not use the same generic words I have used.

For e.g., if your approach has enabled quick wins for a team member, you can't write that generically. Instead you will have to write, 'I am going to enable a quick win in this activity or this project or with this customer by doing the following from my side.' Similarly, if your approach is to empower someone, then don't just write 'empower'. Instead, write, 'I am going to empower my team member to take these three decisions hereafter without consulting me.' Specificity in the plan makes it your plan and makes it actionable. If your plan reads like what I have written in the book, then it is generic and will be difficult to action.

Step 3: Now start to implement your plan with the team. If you have many team members, you could choose a more manageable number to start with, but start with real implementation.

Step 4: Constantly review the results. This is not magic and will not create wonders tomorrow morning, but it will work for sure in three to four months. However, you need to review continuously to first assess if any course correction is required in the plan. And then do a final review after about four months to see what results and learnings you get.

Step 5: Post the review, make a final action plan for how you will implement this in the future in a consistent way.

I hope that as you read this chapter and complete the exercise, you are starting to really see the difference between 'managing the performance' and 'managing the performer'. Managing the performance is a very specific, time-bound process while managing the performer is about how you can manage the person to get the best out of them and also for them to get to their best selves and discover their potential. Many people understand the difference but see a lot of overlaps in both. Hence, it feels like making much ado about nothing. While it may be true that there are similarities, and both are critical for you to become a successful manager, remember that the lever of success this book talks about is 'people management'. Hence, it is important to maintain that the 'people' you work with and the 'performance' they deliver are connected, but both need to be worked on.

Managing the Poor Performer

Let's go back to the LA-LM quadrant of the matrix. We concluded that sometimes, despite our best efforts as managers, we are unable to extract them from that quadrant. That is when managing the poor performer comes in. In managing the poor performer, the word performer is important. We have to make sure we have done all the diligence to ensure that it is indeed the performer who is the problem, and not the environment or the manager or the opportunity, etc. Through a robust process, we must conclude that the performer is indeed the problem. In this process, I would definitely recommend that the manager's manager as well as HR play a role. Once we reach that conclusion, it brings up a very important decision on whether the poor performer should continue to stay in the company or not.

This often also brings an ethical dilemma with it. In many societies, and especially in India, at times, asking someone to leave is considered as being harsh to that individual and possibly impacting their livelihood. Many managers keep delaying this tough decision because of this ethical dilemma. I have personally had to face this dilemma in asking people in my team to leave. Here is my take on it.

Often, when it comes to the ethical dilemma of acting on a poor performer, we get caught in seeing only one point of view—that of the individual. But once we learn to see both points of view—of the individual and the business—the dilemma can be resolved in a clearer manner. Of course, one must be highly humane, respectful and follow all company rules on financial benefits to such individuals.

There is another perspective I want to provide on this. The concept of 'raising the bar'. Teams have to keep raising the bar if they want to stay relevant. If you are not raising your standard of good, then you will soon be left behind and become irrelevant. From 2007 to 2012, Cadbury/Mondelez India had amongst the fastest growth rates for any FMCG company in India. And I am convinced that one of the most important reasons for that was that we raised our bar, our standard of 'what is good' faster than any other FMCG company in the market. As we raised the bar, the bulk of our talent kept pace and raised their own standards as well. But there were a few who struggled to keep up to the new standards and in the most humane and respectful way, we had to take action.

The first two steps are concluding that the performer is indeed the problem and resolving the ethical dilemma in your own head. When faced with such a situation, the right thing is to face the situation and take decisive action following due process. **It is your job and you have to do it**. I do not want to get into the right process of how to do it; each company has its own well-defined process and applying that process in letter and spirit should enable the same. But you have to apply the process; you have to take ownership.

Chapter summary:

1. It is not enough to just manage for performance, but also to manage the performer. As seen in Chapter 3, different stakeholders have different expectations from us and many of these expectations can be met only by managing the performer.
2. Once we start to do that, we transition from being performance managers to talent managers, people who manage both performance and the performer holistically.
3. Successful managers primarily have teams operating in the right half of the Ability-Motivation matrix while less successful ones often end up with a heavier left half.
4. The best way to manage the performer is to plot them on the Ability-Motivation matrix and then tailor your approach based on which quadrant they belong to.
5. A quick summary of your role and approach for each quadrant:

    a. Low Ability-High Motivation: Help them move to the high ability level through coaching, direction and guidance
    b. High Ability-Low Motivation: If career motivation is absent, identify alternate sources of motivation

and deploy. Introspect your role in creating low motivation and correct it.

c. High Ability-High Motivation: Leverage their current high ability to create big impact by providing them with high opportunity and enable career progress.

d. Low Ability-Low Motivation: No one starts in this quadrant; they get here from somewhere else. Finding out why they got here is important. Start by first changing the motivation and then enable them to have small wins and provide active direction to prevent failures.

6. Managing the poor performer:

a. We first have to make sure that it is indeed the performer who is the problem, not the manager or the environment or the opportunity. Post that, we have to overcome the ethical dilemma by recognizing that it is important to look at the second point of view from the perspectives of other team members, organization, etc., and not the just the point of view of the impacted individual. Once you have taken these two steps, you are ready for action.

b. In the action stage, it is important to take ownership as a manager and front the action yourself. It is your job and you must do it.

c. Any action must be humane, respectful to the individual and compliant with the company policies not just in letter, but also in spirit.

6

Performance and the Art
of Delegation

*'I know you are busy, but what I am interested in is what are
you busy about?'—Anonymous*

Delegation has a fairly standard definition. It is the shifting
of responsibility and authority for specific functions/
tasks/decisions from a leader or manager to another team
member.

In the last two chapters, we spoke a lot about
performance from all angles—how a manager can
impact team members' performance, how we look at
performance from the perspective of the performer,
etc. Another aspect very clearly linked to performance is
that of delegation. Delegating to your team members is
a vital skill in being a good manager. It is a word which
is often used loosely and most managers perceive that
they delegate well to their team members. It is often
interesting to talk to a manager and hear them say
that they delegate a lot to their team members, they

empower them, etc. And then you talk to that manager's team members and hear exactly the opposite about how the manager hardly lets go of anything; how they want to know everything and that there is limited freedom for team members. This is a story that gets repeated in many companies. A great symptom of poor delegation is when team members are eternally lining up near the manager's office for time and the manager does not have enough time for all of them. It creates an illusory sense of a highly important manager, but it is really a symptom of poor delegation. In my judgement, most managers delegate less than they should be doing. I want to first explain to you why it is good for you as a manager to delegate more, not less. There is a mistaken notion about delegation we have—we think that when we delegate as a manager, we are doing the team member a favour. That is incorrect. When you delegate to your team member, **you do yourself a favour as a manager and not the team member.** I shall explain the logic behind that in the next few pages.

In *Catalyst,* there is a chapter on personal productivity where I describe a concept called 'Rocks first'. I will give a very brief overview here, but would urge readers to read *Catalyst*, if they want to get the full picture. Basically, at a very macro level, there are two kinds of work we do, what I call important and high impact and less important and less impact. For purposes of simplicity, I use the word 'rocks' to describe the important work and 'sand' to describe the less important work. In *Catalyst,* I had argued that the more a person focuses on the rocks and less on the sand, the more productive and successful the person becomes. But the single biggest barrier to that is that the sand cannot be left unattended and hence, our usual approach becomes, 'Let's get over with the sand first and then, when I get some free time, I shall turn my focus towards the rocks.' And you know what? **That free time never comes—the sand keeps flowing.**

When I talk to people, I often hear things like, 'I need to prepare the market launch plan for the new product, but I am so busy right now. I am going to finish all of what I am doing and once I get free, I shall get to the launch plan.' There is also the famous activity called hiring which everyone is involved in. A manager has a vacancy in their team; HR identifies a candidate and then the manager says, 'I am very tied up right now. Let us schedule the interview after two weeks.' When, as a manager, you have a vacancy, then filling that vacancy is one of the most important priorities. A vacancy hurts your performance and your company's performance. Yet, we are so busy with the sand that we can't find the time for the interview, a high priority activity.

What I am describing happens everywhere; it's not just you and me who suffer from this problem. Most people do. And that is because it is natural for us to enjoy the feeling of being busy. When we accomplish a lot of small things in a day, there is a sense of satisfaction we derive—an 'I did a lot today' kind of feeling and that keeps attracting us. If there is sand around, most of us will naturally choose sand—it feels easy, tangible, actionable and shows some immediate impact and satisfaction. If from that situation, we have to get our focus to the rocks, there is only one way to getting there—get rid of all the sand from your plate. Make the sand someone else's responsibility. That is where delegation comes in.

There is often another obstacle to delegation—when a manager feels the team member is 'not ready' for the delegated task. I hear this very often—this bias towards 'non-readiness' of team members. While there may be some truth to it, the question here is—how will the less experienced team members EVER be ready for delegation if the practice is not started? Also, they may be doing it in a different way—their way—which may not be acceptable to the manager since they may have an inherent bias towards the way they have been doing things. Hence, the team member feels less and less confident in handling the delegated task. This is a tough one to handle and requires a lot of openness on the part of the manager to delegate to their team members.

I can think of a way out here—there are two things that help. One, choose simpler, smaller tasks, the 'low hanging fruits', that are more operational and don't require much deviation from the standard. Once the team member has performed these kinds of tasks well, their confidence in themselves increases, as well as the manager's confidence in their ability to do greater tasks. Two, sit with the member you are delegating to, and clearly define the 'outcome' you want, not the 'way it should be done'. This helps in alignment and better performance of the delegated task. I will talk more about it in the 'what' and 'how' of delegation.

My simple motto about delegation that I want to leave you with is '**Delegate more than what you feel comfortable with',** and release more time for yourself for the 'rocks'.

There are two other benefits to delegation as well. One is that it improves the speed and agility of the system. When people have to keep checking back, it automatically slows things down as compared to if they can just decide and go ahead without having to get your approval for everything. As a manager, if your team is operating with speed and agility, then it will definitely outperform other teams and bring you a good reputation.

And of course, there is the benefit of energizing your team and motivating them to feel empowered. When team members feel they can make decisions, they take greater ownership; they are more accountable and much more engaged in their jobs. You will have a team of tigers who are raring to go. So go ahead, delegate, delegate and delegate.

The 'what' and 'how' of delegation

Currently, the process by which delegation happens can, at best, be described as serendipity or accidental. It happens in a very organic way between a manager and a team member and is often a function of their personalities. Of course, there are a small set of topics, maybe 10 per cent of decisions for which companies create 'authority matrix' or 'approval rights', etc. These things mainly pertain to financial and control areas. Over 90 per cent of decisions taken between the manager and the team member do not have any formal delegation; they only have delegation by precedent or evolution, a classical Darwinian model.

Hence, one would often see that if you compare two sets of managers and team members in similar roles, say the North Zonal manager (the Delhi head) and their team members versus the South Zonal manager (the Bengaluru head) and their team members, you will find that there are differences in delegation. The Delhi manager may have delegated decisions A, B and C to their team members while the Bengaluru manager will have only delegated decision A to their team members. This despite both sets of people being in similar roles. This is what I mean by delegation happening in an evolutionary and accidental manner. *I am a firm believer that delegation must be planned, not accidental, and must be formal, not informal.* Let me describe the process I recommend you use as a manager to delegate.

'What' to delegate

Here is where most of us need to make a 180-degree turn in our thinking. Today, the thinking about delegation is based on 'what my team member is capable of doing' and then delegating those things slowly with supervision. From there, our thinking has to change based on what I wrote about in the initial portion of the delegation section—the main purpose of delegation is to give yourself the time and space to do important things. Hence, you have to judge your capacity to do important things and post that, delegate whatever you don't have the capacity for. Hence, your capacity to do important things should be the primary driver of the delegation, not the capability of your team member. Occasionally, there may be a team member who is genuinely not capable. That is either a hiring mistake or a talent mistake which must be fixed, and not a delegation error.

Once you change this thinking by 180 degrees, then I recommend that you divide all the decisions/activities that need to be done into three lists:

1. Things I want to drive myself, because they are very important and high impact
2. Things my team members can drive, but can consult me if they want to
3. Things that my team members can drive and I don't want to be consulted on

Once you make this matrix, you will see that effectively all of the decisions and activities under the second and third lists can be delegated. One thing to watch out for here is the tendency of managers to put too many things under the first list so as to avoid delegating. Please do not put more items under the first list than you have the capacity to handle. As I said before, the motto is '**Delegate more than what you are comfortable with**.'

Let me give you an example of the time when I was the marketing head at Cadbury/Mondelez. We used to do a significant amount of advertising, digital marketing, activations, etc., and for each campaign, this entailed many activities, many pieces of design, and many decisions. I realized that if I got involved in every single item, then I would lose sight of the big picture and the important things.

Hence, this is the delegation matrix I made:

- *Things I want to drive myself*: Overall campaign strategy and the main advertisement that would go on television

- *Things my team members can do and consult me if they want to*: Press advertising, radio advertising, digital marketing
- *Things my team members can do and do not need to consult me*: All activations, outdoor media, media innovations and any other part of the campaign

'How' to delegate

Once you have a clear list of what to delegate, comes the important part: how to delegate. This is crucial because this is about behaviours and establishing confidence in the team. Many a time, I notice that people delegate on paper, but don't really delegate in practice because they don't get the 'how' right. Delegation is complete only when your team members are making decisions confidently without checking back with you. If they don't have the confidence to make the decisions, then the delegation is incomplete. To get there, one has to focus on three important aspects of the 'how'—i) formality, ii) clarity of communication, and iii) post delegation behaviour.

The first part is a formality

Extending my example from above, what I chose to do was share with my marketing team the delegation matrix that I had determined earlier regarding marketing activities, and clearly informed them that this was how we would operate from then on. Absolute formality in black and white, not an informal chat over lunch or a casual conversation suggesting that they do something, etc.

It was communication through a formal email to the team, clearly delegating what they could do with no ambiguity. Once you get your three lists in the matrix ready, I recommend sending exactly the same kind of clear, formal communication to the team. It prevents you from backtracking and gives them the confidence that you really mean it and are not just saying it for the sake of saying it.

Next is clarity of communication

Clear communication is necessary, on how one will operate with each of the three lists. Here is what I communicated as the ways of working with the team for the three lists that I had put together.

Things I want to drive myself: The team obviously does the groundwork, prepares and analyses the data, comes up with ideas, but engages me at each important stage. Hence, on something in this list, the team would engage with me regularly; I would provide inputs at each stage and the final decision would be mine.

Things they can drive and consult me on, if they want: These are things that they were free to do entirely by themselves. But at any point, if they wanted my opinion, they could consult me. However, the consultation was under two conditions:

1. It was not mandatory for them to accept my opinion.
2. If they accepted my opinion and things didn't go well, it did not become my problem, it remained their problem.

Things they can drive and I don't even want to be consulted on:
These are things they would do completely by themselves.
Even if they came to me for an opinion, I would refuse to
give them one.

Finally, post-delegation behaviour

Often, we might have put something on the second or
third lists but our behaviour with the team on those items
might not change. Let me share some of the behaviours
I had to practise consciously to institutionalize this.
I remember sitting in my cabin one day when a senior
team member, Anil Viswanathan, walked in with a press
ad that was going to get released and asked me to okay it.
I remember telling him, 'Anil, this is in list two. It is your
decision, my friend, not mine.' He then asked me for my
opinion. I gave him my opinion, but clearly told him that
he was not required to go by it. In this kind of a situation,
it is easy to fall back on old habits and behaviours. If, at
this point, we take the decision in our hands because the
team member came to us, then we will kill the delegation
process then and there. It is vital that we practise what
we put down on paper. It requires conscious effort and
memory on our part to build this kind of delegation into
the system and ensure it does not turn into delegation in
name only. Of course, Anil being Anil, took his decision
and went ahead, and it is not an accident that he is one of
the foremost marketers in India today.

The other kind of discomfort I had to overcome in that
delegation process was my boss asking me questions on
things I did not know because I had delegated that activity.

Because I had delegated, I truly did not know enough to answer his questions and had to often tell him, 'Anand, I have to check and come back to you.' Sometimes, this discomfort, of not knowing everything when the boss asks makes people not delegate. It is important to overcome that discomfort and be able to tell the boss, 'I will come back'. And when you do go back, take your team member along and let them truly represent their work.

I hope the above pages have given you an in-depth view into delegation. More often than not, that word is used casually and everyone thinks they delegate well. But as you understand more and more, based on what I have written, you start to figure out that delegation is not just an action, but a process. It is a culture that needs to be nurtured and built. One of the foremost jobs of a good manager is to build that process and culture of delegation and empowerment in their teams. Empowered teams perform exceptionally well and make managers shine while never forgetting the fact that the time you liberate for yourself to do what is important is what makes you shine even more.

In my Lead & Manage workshops, after having said all the above and with the bulk of the group nodding their heads in agreement, right at the end of the session, one solitary hand will pop up with a question without fail. That question would be, 'What if I delegate and things go wrong? Won't I be in trouble?' This is one of the great unsaid barriers to delegation—what if my team member messes it up? I typically answer it by asking a few questions.

1. Do you have the capacity to do everything yourself? If yes, you don't need to delegate. In fact, you don't even need a team. If no, then you have to delegate, there is no option.
2. Once you decide to delegate, let's assume that some things will go wrong. Would you rather that the things that go wrong are the important things or less important things?

Usually, these two questions do help in bringing even the more cynical ones across the finish line, and I hope it has brought home those of you who still had delegation anxiety.

I will share with you one last trick of mine which I practised as I delegated. It is based on a phrase I picked up from someone else: 'Eyes on, hands off'. It means that I could often spot trouble well before it blew up. As I delegated, I had some time on my hands and would use it to be on top of the situation. I would see all sales reports; seek and go through brand scorecards, key market research reports, etc. I did all this without troubling my team because this kind of information was available easily. This meant that my finger was on the pulse. I did not have to take every decision but I would keep track if the business was going in the right direction and if I ever had a concern, I would simply shoot a question. Again, it was shooting a question, not taking the decision in my hands.

So dear friends, if you want to be super successful, delegate more than you are comfortable with and then focus your time on doing the important things with a big picture view through 'Eyes on, hands off'.

Exercise:

Throughout this book, we have been using exercises to connect the concepts in this book to your reality. If you do not do that, you will enjoy reading, and will appreciate it intellectually. But after a few days, it will be gone with the wind. It would not have made a difference to your effectiveness as a manager. So here is another exercise for you to convert a concept into reality to make you more effective.

This exercise is to actually make a delegation plan and execute it.

Step 1: 'What' to delegate. Make the three lists: things that I want to drive myself; things that my team can drive that they can consult me on if they want, and things that my team can drive and I don't even want to be consulted on. Make sure you cover the bulk of what you are involved in. An incomplete list still results in a lot of spillover work on your table.

Step 2: Prepare the 'how' plan.

-   What will be your formal communication method and date? Are you going to call a team meeting and formally announce to them followed by an email?
-   What is the clarity you can provide on ways of working for each of the three lists in that meeting?
-   What post delegation behaviours are you consciously going to follow yourself? How will you overcome delegation anxiety?

-   What will you do with your free time now? Don't let
    new sand come in. Make a focused plan to attack the
    rocks. Make a plan for 'Eyes on, hands off' without
    disturbing the team.

Step 3: Execute the plan. Don't look back. No anxiety
and pangs. Just execute.

In a few months, you will find that you are a more effective
and successful manager. Happy delegating!

Chapter summary:

1. Most managers think they delegate well. But talk to
    their team members and you get a different story.
    Most of us under-delegate.
2. Benefits of delegation:
    a) To create time and space for yourself to do
        important and impactful things which otherwise
        always get left out due to the sand in our
        workplaces.
    b) To increase speed and agility in your team.
    c) To create an empowered and energized team which
        will then take accountability and outperform other
        teams, making you shine as a manager.

3. It is important to realize that when we delegate, we
    don't do our teams a favour. In fact, we do a favour to
    ourselves. The motto of delegation must be, 'Delegate
    more than what you feel comfortable with.'
4. Currently, 'what' we delegate is more accidental and
    evolutionary. From there, we have to move to a more

deliberate set of what to delegate by dividing all our activities into three different lists:

a) Things I want to drive myself.
b) Things I want the team to drive, but they can consult me on these things, if they want to.
c) Things I want the team to drive and don't even want to be consulted on.

All the items in lists two and three can be delegated.

5. There are three aspects to the 'how' of delegation:
    a) Be formal, not informal. Call a formal meeting, send a formal mail or a note. Put your delegation list out there transparently to your team.
    b) Be clear in 'ways of working' communication for each of the three lists.
    c) Have disciplined post delegation behaviours. Do not lapse into old habits of taking control.

    Once you delegate, there will be things you won't know. If your boss asks a question, don't be afraid to say, 'I will come back.'

6. Overcome the ultimate delegation anxiety of what will happen if things go wrong after you delegate by asking these two questions to yourself:
    a) Do I have the capacity to do everything myself? If not, I have to delegate.
    b) If things have to go wrong, would I rather that important high impact stuff goes wrong or less important things go wrong?

7. Develop an 'Eyes on, hands off' capability to predict trouble before it happens.

7

Managing Teams

In the previous three chapters, we discussed how to go about managing individual team members. Suppose you have six individuals in your team and you do a terrific job of managing them as individuals. Does that mean you are creating an effective team? I want you to spend a few minutes thinking about what it takes beyond managing individuals in creating a team. Jot down the points here:

1.

2.

3.

Before we discuss what it takes to make a good team, let us discuss when we can consider a team to be a good one. Let us go to our favourite analogy: sporting teams. There are very big sporting leagues around the world—football leagues in Europe with many teams; the basketball league in the US and of course, the famous IPL cricket league in India. As you are aware, players can be part of any team based on a complex process of bidding and auctions as well as transfer deals. Let us look at it from a player's lens and assess when a team would be considered a good one.

Assume that the player inherently has the potential to perform at X level by themselves. The player joins team A and continues to perform at X level. In the next season, the player joins team B and their performance drops to 70 per cent of X. In the year after that, the player joins team C and their performance improves to 150 per cent of X. That, in my opinion, is the simplest indicator of whether a team is a good team or a poor team—does it amplify the player's performance or does it diminish it? When a team is such that it can amplify an individual player's performance beyond what they normally do, then that team can be characterized as a good team.

The same thing applies to the teams you and I manage in the corporate world. Are we, as managers, creating teams which amplify the individual's performance from their normal levels or is it the opposite where individuals fail to perform even at their normal levels? Take a look at your team and then ask yourself the question: 'Are the members of my team performing above or below their inherent normal levels?' Reflect on this for a while; think of a few of your team members and honestly answer this question: by virtue of being in your team, has their performance improved compared to if they had been in another team or has their performance worsened compared to if they had been in another team? Sometimes, there is a tendency to cherry-pick in this reflection and choose only those team members whose performance is good. Hence, we may start to think that the team is effective. So, please take a cross section of people to make sure you get a good, honest reflection on the kind of team you have created.

As a manager and team leader, you have one job—to create a team dynamic that 'amplifies' individual performance. By creating and managing such an amplifier team, managers can become team amplifiers. And it is important to understand that simply managing individuals effectively does not mean we are being team amplifiers. Building an amplifier team requires a set of actions from our side that is over and above managing individuals.

There is a lot of literature available on creating and building teams and I don't want to cover all of that. I am going to choose the four aspects that I think have the greatest impact on creating amplifier teams. These are: i) aligned priorities, ii) collective purpose, iii) relationships, and iv) review processes.

1. Aligning the team's priorities

The starting point for a good team is whether it is **aligned** on where it is going, i.e., direction, strategy and key priorities. Going back to sports, one team in cricket might have a strategy of being aggressive in the early overs and then playing conservatively in the middle while another team might have the exact opposite strategy. Both are legitimate strategies—the more important question is whether everyone in the team is aligned to one strategy and are they willing to play their part in it. This alignment ensures that every team member is thinking along the same axis, and in the same direction when they play.

Similarly, as managers, a very important task we play in building an amplifier team is in building alignment— of direction, strategy and priorities. The key word is *building*. We are not simply deciding and communicating the direction and strategy of the team, that does not create alignment. We have to build these with the team, and once the team has ownership and alignment, they function effectively.

Alignment helps individual team members amplify their performance in the following ways:

1. Many a time, we have been in teams where another team member is actually pulling in the opposite direction. Taking the above example of a sports team, can you imagine a situation where the team has a strategy of being aggressive in the beginning, but one of the opening batsmen actually ends up playing defensively all the time? In such a situation, a lot of our time and energy actually goes in convincing or neutralizing their opposite move. In an aligned team, we would not have such a problem. The bulk of our time and energy would be productively deployed in getting work done rather than countering another team member.

2. As a new team member, it is very easy to come up to speed in an aligned team very quickly. And this helps the individual member to focus on enhancing their own performance much more.

2. Creating collective purpose

The second aspect that we, as managers and team leaders, have to create is a **collective purpose**. I remember when I was a young branch manager in 1995 in Rajasthan in Asian Paints. It was the month of August, traditionally the biggest month for paint sales as it just precedes Diwali. Traders would buy and stock heavily for the upcoming Diwali sales. In August of 1994, the branch had sold 570 tons of paint. Being a young, brash manager, I visualized an ambitious target for myself—I said we would do 1000 tons during the same period in 1995, a growth of 75 per cent over the previous year. In any logical, mature business, this would look like an absurd target and possibly impossible to execute. But as a branch, we did it because we managed to make it a mission, a zealous purpose among ourselves. How did I go about building the purpose? The first job was to get the branch team together across all the functions—sales, logistics, accounts, IT, etc.—and create belief. I presented the usual analytics that any good manager gives to explain why something is possible. Then, I unveiled some unique strategies to begin to create belief. But the real breakthrough came when I did two things:

1. I asked them to discuss among themselves and come up with what they needed for achieving the goal of 1000 tons. I agreed to everything they asked because it was all perfectly logical. That transferred ownership.
2. Then came the interesting part—the state of Rajasthan; its history of Rajputs, their valour and

ability to fight against all odds. In Asian Paints those days, Mumbai, Bengaluru, Delhi, Ahmedabad, etc. were the important branches, Rajasthan was not so important. So, when we invoked collective pride by saying, 'Let us show others what the Rajasthan team is made of and the history we come from', it created a sense of zealous purpose, which proved to be fantastic.

We actually did 1000 tons that August, possibly one of the most exhilarating months in my thirty-year working life. But the real joy was not in just achieving that number. It was in seeing how a collective sense of purpose and pride can transform a regular team into a pack of go-getting tigers. It was this period, early in my career, when I understood the power of collective pride and purpose when it comes to building and transforming teams.

Purpose can be of many kinds. The one I described was more short-term, but you can also create a sense of purpose for the longer term. It can be around achievements; or about being the best or about making a difference. The source can be from anywhere. But the important thing as a manager is to create a collective purpose and pride in your team, a purpose that lifts your team and allows each team member to put that extra energy and intensity into every day as well as enjoy the journey.

3. Fostering strong relationships

The third driver to creating great teams is **relationships**. This is not the relationship between you and your team members, which, of course, is important, but these are relationships between team members themselves. There is a lot of research nowadays which seems to suggest that relationships might be the most important drivers for effective teams. Now, 'relationship' is one of those words—no one believes that their relationships are bad or that their team members' relationships are poor. It is one of those things we assume will automatically fall into place with time. But if you want to create a great team, better than other teams, then you cannot just wait for things to fall into place.

Let us start by articulating what we would call a good relationship. I would use the term *personal chemistry* as the key to a good relationship. In any role, there are several colleagues we have to work with, and we develop working relationships with all of them. But when you want to create a great team, then working relationships are not enough. All teams already have those, so it doesn't make your team different, and hence better. That working relationship must change to personal chemistry between your team members. That is when the relationship matures and starts to form the backbone of a great team. Now this is a bit of an antithesis to today's modern world where 'professional' is the operative word. There are distinct efforts to separate the personal from the professional. I am not advocating that we become unprofessional, i.e., I won't say that as a colleague I will only work with you if I have a personal connection with you, otherwise I won't. I think being professional is a basic requirement. We must do what is necessary to support our colleagues with what they need. But equally, I am convinced that simply being professional does not create magical teams. Such teams get created when there is a degree of personal chemistry amongst the team members, a desire to see each other succeed, a willingness to support someone who is in trouble beyond what is required professionally, a sense of comfort and joy in working together, etc.

As a manager, the immediate question that follows is, 'How do I facilitate building this personal chemistry amongst my team members?' I have three tips for that: i) travelling together whenever possible, ii) family connections, and iii) spending time discussing things other than work. These things provide opportunities to find connecting points beyond just work for team members, which they can build their relationship around. As a manager, if you can facilitate each of the above on a continuous basis, you would be surprised at how rapidly the personal chemistry between your team starts to build up.

4. Proper review processes

The fourth aspect is the regular **reviews** that you will be conducting with your teams to monitor their work and performance. How a manager conducts review meetings involving team members can often make or break great teams. All the hard work done in building alignment, collective purpose and relationships can be undone by one bad review meeting which pits people against each other as adversaries.

At a very broad level, I have observed team leaders conduct two kinds of review meetings. In one kind, the team leader basically uses the meeting to review each individual team member in the presence of other team members. In the other kind, the team leader and the team members collectively review the business and try to solve problems. The first kind of review meeting is usually a destroyer of team spirit and fabric. In such meetings, one team member gets pushed into a corner and, in a desperate attempt to wriggle out they will throw the ball at another team member and so on. The ball throwing continues till the bulk of deposits in the relationship bank is emptied in one meeting. The other kind of meeting, where the team leader and team members collectively review the business and the problems at hand, becomes more productive as it builds a team identity. It sends a message that problems must be solved by all of us, throwing the ball at each other won't do. It builds overall team ownership for all issues rather than narrow ownership of just what is in each person's domain. So, as a team leader, try and move your team meetings to the second kind. If you want to review a team member, then a collective team meeting is not the place for it, one-to-one is the right way to do it.

These four aspects—aligned priorities, collective pride and purpose, relationships and review processes—are key facilitators that you as a manager and a team leader can act on to build a great team, an amplifier team that helps each team member perform better than their normal. I have had the privilege of working under two master team builders—Bharat Puri and Anand Kripalu. Here are my observations of how I saw them do it, so you too can benefit from it.

The master team builders

Both Bharat and Anand were master team builders, possibly the best. But the interesting thing was that both had their own unique styles when it came to team building. While they did all the regular things that were required like alignment, collective purpose, relationships and reviews, they had their own unique contributions that truly made a difference.

Where Bharat stood out among other team leaders was in relationships. Any team of his always enjoyed outstanding relationships with each other and his teams were always the envy of other teams. Early on in my career, as a bachelor, when I was a brand manager in Asian Paints and he was the head of marketing, at least once a week, he would round up the few of us in the bachelor gang and take us home for dinner spontaneously. His wonderful wife, Alka, no less a person than Bharat in many ways, would make us feel at home every time. I lost count of how often I ate at their home in the three–four years of my bachelorhood—not less than 100 times. Sometimes, when I think about where my deep personal loyalty to Bharat comes from, I do think it goes back to those days and those dinners. Bharat, knowing that the marketing team was very young, and most of us were very middle class in those days, would go out of his way to introduce us to new experiences, be it going to concerts as a team or watching live sports together or for that matter horse racing. We all learnt a lot of new things outside of work, and that was due to the efforts he made. As a result, that marketing team was one team; we were friends with each other and some of them remain my best friends even three decades since. You can imagine how seamlessly we worked—people would back each other up, favours were asked and given easily, an important project for one person was everyone's project and so on. And years later, even as a managing director of a large corporation, that trait of building strong relationships has been continued by Bharat. At offsite meetings, during the late-night sessions where we would sit together (adda) and talk about anything and everything under the moon, further enabled by Bharat's ability to truly make himself feel like one of us and not some elusive boss—those were things that led the team to build deep bonds with each other. Whatever be the challenges, everyone in Bharat's team always knows that they can bank on the rest of the team, their friends.

Anand's strength was in alignment and reviews. His ability to get the team together and agree to a set of aligned priorities was phenomenal. He believed in 'fewer is better'. It was all the more challenging to get the team together to prune the list of priorities to as few as possible, but he always did it. In Anand's team, we never worked at cross purposes with each other; priorities were owned by everyone. Further, it was his way of running review meetings that taught me the simple tenet—**the purpose of review meetings is to solve problems, not review people**. His ability to sit back in a review meeting, toss the problem at the team and let them jostle with it, without the urge to take it back into his hands, was extraordinary. He would step in towards the end when required, but most of the time, he would gently steer as the team owned the problem and solved for it. This combination of aligned priorities and a team that collectively owned business problems resulted in one of the most effective leadership teams I have worked in. Both Anand and I joined Cadbury/Mondelez in 2005 when the company's turnover was approximately Rs 570 crore. By the time Anand left in 2013, it was close to Rs 5000 crore. That is the power of creating a unified team, which could align itself to high targets, prioritize and build strategies towards achieving those high targets and collectively solve for any problems that came in the way.

As you can see from these master team builders, working on the basics is important. All four aspects: alignment, collective purpose, relationships and reviews were things both did well. But the extraordinary teams they created came from not just doing the basics well; it came from their strengths, truly unique and authentic to them as leaders. So, as you set yourself to building extraordinary teams, do the basics well, but think about what is your authentic trait as a team leader. Happy team building!

Chapter summary:

1. Managing individuals in your team does not mean you are managing the team. Managing the team requires a separate set of activities.
2. The purpose of managing the team is to make your team an amplifier team, which amplifies the performance of team members by virtue of being in this team as opposed to being in any other team.
3. There are four drivers to creating amplifier teams: aligned priorities, collective pride and purpose, relationships and review process.

    a. Alignment is making sure that all your team members are aligned to the same direction, strategies and priorities. Many teams work at cross purposes to each other and alignment is crucial to prevent that.
    b. Collective pride and purpose are about having a sense of missionary zeal which allows each team member to put in that little bit of extra intensity and focus.
    c. Relationships between team members are all about personal chemistry. It is about going beyond working professional relationships to caring and supporting each other and taking pride in each other's success.
    d. A review process where the team leader uses the meeting to review each member of the team in the presence of other team members often destroys team dynamics. Instead, a good review process is

one where the team leader and the members are collectively reviewing the business and solving problems. The purpose of review meetings is to solve problems, not review people.

4. Good work on all the four aspects can help you build a good team. But over and above the good work on the four, if you can build a spike in one of them to an extraordinary level, then you would become a master team builder.

Summary: Section 2 and Introduction to Section 3

In our quest to become better leaders and managers, in Section 1, we spoke about the need to make four broad shifts:

1. *From* thinking of ourselves as either leader or manager
    To understanding that everyone has to do both.
2. *From* focusing on the position/title
    To focusing on the action—actually leading and managing irrespective of the position.
3. *From* having double standards where we have higher expectations from our managers and leaders than what we are doing for our team
    To reversing that and focusing first on becoming a great leader and manager for our teams, irrespective of what our leaders and managers are doing.
4. *From* meeting only a few expectations of a limited set of stakeholders
    To meeting multiple expectations that all stakeholders have from us as leaders and managers.

These four shifts set us up to become the great leader and manager we want to be—someone who is holistic, has high impact well beyond the position and someone who is positively impacting their team and the wider organization.

In Section 2, we then moved our attention to how to become a good manager. As per our definition, managing is the art of impacting people by being directly involved. We identified the key areas where we are directly involved in managing our teams and how can we do a great job of that. The key shifts that we have to undertake to become great at managing are:

1. *From* asking for better performance
   To driving better performance by understanding the core drivers of performance using the PAMOD framework
2. *From* being only performance managers
   To becoming talent managers who manage both the performance and the performer.
3. *From* being ineffective at poor performer management
   To taking full ownership and being effective and highly humane in poor performer management.
4. *From* under-delegating and having a lot of delegation anxiety
   To delegating more than you are comfortable with using the right techniques of 'what' and 'how' of delegation.
5. *From* just managing individuals
   To building amplifying teams.

Making these five shifts will transform you into absolutely superb managers; our impact on our people while being directly involved will be exceptional and this will set you up for a great career ahead.

The next big step is to master leading—the art of impacting people without being directly involved. I had given a few examples of this in Chapter 1, but I do want to give a few more examples here to enliven this further.

At one level, leadership can be simply about inspiring people. A leader could make a speech to a very large audience and inspire so significantly that it impacts them and what they do subsequently. At another level, it could be about proclamations and strategies. A leader in a large IT company with over 1,00,000 employees could say, 'We are going to bring hazardous e-waste to zero.' Now, the leader might have worked directly with a few people to formulate a strategy for that, but by making a proclamation like this, the 1,00,000+ employees that the leader has not interacted with directly would also begin making their own plans to bring down e-waste by themselves. The leader is impacting all the 1,00,000+ employees in this manner.

The above two examples are what can be called pure leading examples. The more complex type is where a leader leads through the act of managing. I had given one example in Chapter 1, now let me try and give one more example here to land that concept better as it is a very important part of leadership. Let us say there is a leader of a very large airport, which sees millions of passengers pass through daily. One day, on a walk around the airport, the leader spots some water spilled on the floor. Immediately, they call for the staff and personally supervise the cleaning of the floor till it is sparkling again. This is an act of managing. The leader spotted a problem, directly got involved with a set of people and solved it. However, there is a leading message here which is hidden in the leader's behaviour. And the message is that any spillage or dirt, however small, is not acceptable at the airport. They are not directly saying that to the people but demonstrating it through actions. The people infer that message as well and the next time they notice a small spillage, they might act on it immediately, compared to the past when they might have overlooked it. The leader did not tell them that. They did not say, 'Next time you notice something, act on it.' Instead, their action—what they did when they noticed the spillage—had that indirect impact on all the people and will impact and change their behaviour in the future.

As we seek to become great leaders and lead well, we must master both kinds of leadership actions. The first kind are what I call *leading by doing,* which is about doing a specific set of things purely to have leading impact—purely to impact people who you are not directly involved with. The second kind is what I call *leading by being* which is by impacting people indirectly with everything you do and by impacting people through your nature and the human being you are. We shall cover both these in the next section in our attempt to master leading and leadership.

SECTION 3

8

Transform from Just Managing to 'Managing + Leading'

If I were to set up a contest ranking the most loosely defined, most jargon-like words in the management lexicon, I have a sneaking suspicion that 'leadership' would win that contest or come somewhere near the top. It is one of those words which acts as a catch-all. Sometimes I like to call such words 'motherhood words'. Even wishing a colleague happy birthday and shaking their hand warmly can be considered leadership; rolling up one's sleeves and spending nine hours with three people and preparing a presentation is also leadership; being willing to sit in the backseat of a car with three people as opposed to two can also be called great leadership at times. As of now, thankfully, visiting the washroom a few times a day has not been called leadership. But I wouldn't be surprised if it eventually does feature on that list.

Sorry for the sarcasm, but it does get the point across— in today's world, anything and everything can be thrown under the word leadership. *In a way, what has happened is that instead of defining leadership and acts of leadership, the world has moved to defining leaders.* And once a person is defined as a leader, then whatever they do is leadership, whether it meets the criteria of leadership or not. **This simplification of 'actions of leaders = leadership' is the greatest disservice done to the art and science of leadership, and in many ways, it has resulted in potentially poorer leadership over time**. Leadership has certain standards, certain definitions, and everything a leader does is not automatically leadership.

This problem has been accentuated further by companies and HR departments lowering the bar on whom they call leaders. A few decades ago, the CEO and one level below them were called leaders. But slowly and steadily, there is a downward creep, and today, in the average company, even those five–six levels below the CEO too are sometimes called leaders. Continuing in my tone of sarcasm, I am willing to hazard a guess that sometime in the next decade, entry-level trainees will also start being called leaders. My primary problem is not with people being called leaders. As you know, my view is that everyone must lead irrespective of whether they are called a leader or not, and more people being called leaders does not negatively impact that. My greater problem is with the fact that instead of understanding and defining real leadership, we have simplified leadership to 'actions of people called leaders = leadership'. Instead of defining leadership and asking leaders to stand up and deliver to that standard, we have simply reversed the game in an undesirable way and stated that whatever they do as leaders is leadership. In my opinion, this reversal has the potential to lower the understanding and standard of leadership over time. That is one of the reasons I have spent a lot of time trying to formulate and perfect the definitions of leading and managing for this book.

Defining leadership based on the 'why' of leadership

To understand and define leadership, let us start with understanding the 'why' of leadership. Let us start with that one person who no one would quibble about being called a leader—the CEO/MD of the company, the number one top person. How does a CEO deliver their own performance? Further, in many ways, the CEO's performance is equal to the company's performance. Hence, one can broaden this question to 'how does a CEO deliver their own performance as well as the company's performance?' If you look at a CEO's diary/calendar and do an analysis of where they spend their time, in most cases, you will find that it goes into acts of managing— actions they are directly involved in, mostly with their direct team. It would include activities like annual budgeting/planning, financial planning and forecasting, strategy, being involved in senior level people/talent decisions, mergers/acquisitions/alliances/collaborations, crisis management, high-level government and regulatory interface, etc. If you look at most of these, they would be managing actions, actions the CEOs are directly and deeply involved in. However, if we go back to the core question, 'how does a CEO deliver their as well as the company's performance', then you will find that these managing actions that they spend the bulk of their time on possibly impacts only 10–20 per cent of the performance of the company. The bulk of the performance of the company happens due to what hundreds and thousands of employees do on a daily basis and that is not something the CEO is directly involved in. Effectively, you can say that the CEO is not in direct control of the bulk of the performance of the company.

Now, as a CEO, I can have two points of view when approaching this situation. One would be a passive approach—managing the performance of the company is why organizational structures, managers and processes exist. The second view is a more active approach—I want to impact performance that's beyond my control and sight. Let's take the passive approach first. As a CEO, I believe that there are many important things I need to do (take all the activities listed in the previous paragraph) and that is where the bulk of my attention should go. There is the full organization, comprising layers of managers, each actively managing the next level and further, there are organizational processes to manage the rest. That combination of managers and processes should deliver the company's performance by itself. I need to focus on those actions that only a CEO can do—after all, a lower-level manager cannot decide on strategy or on an acquisition, so I need to focus on such key managing actions. Now, this is a perfectly legitimate approach and has some validity to it. It is capable of delivering steady and acceptable performance, particularly in efficient organizations with good managers and processes. But my own guess is that this approach will never drive a magical and transformational change in performance, and I want to give you a non-corporate analogy on why I say so.

Let us consider a war scenario and look at the chief of the army—the general—who spends all their time in the war room taking decisions on strategies, troop and armament deployment, coordinating with the navy, air force and the government, etc. All of these are activities only a general can do; a lower-level army officer won't be able to do them. The general is so consumed doing these things that they leave the running of the rest of the army operations, motivating the troops, etc., to the field commanders. Now imagine another general who says, 'Yes, I need to do these things, but I also need to find time for motivating the troops on the frontline. I will make surprise visits to forward bases and motivate them; I shall send them inspiring messages every day', etc. Who do you think would be the more effective general during the war situation? The one who says, 'I will do my job and the rest of the organization will do theirs', or the one who says, 'Apart from what the rest of the organizational hierarchy and processes ensure, I will try and have some impact on every troop member'? In my mind, the answer is obvious, and I would assume in your mind too.

So, ignoring the passive approach, the other approach a CEO can take is the active approach, which says that while the bulk of the company's performance is not in my direct control, I do want to impact it positively in whichever way I can. That is where leadership comes in and the act of leading comes in. *This is the 'why' of leadership, the need to impact and influence what is important to you but is not in your direct involvement or control.*

Let us go back to the definitions that we gave for leading and managing in Chapter 1.

Managing: The art of impacting people while being directly involved.

Leading: The art of impacting people without being directly involved.

The first and the biggest transformation I want you to make is to erase the notion that everything a leader does is leadership, and instead imbibe the new thought—leadership is a deliberate set of actions which has a goal of positively impacting those people and actions where one's involvement is low. Anything that doesn't achieve that objective is not leadership, even if done by a person called a leader.

If a CEO wants to impact the wider expanse of people and performance in the organization, then they have to go to the definition of leading as given above. They have to learn the art of impacting people where they are not directly involved. They cannot have the simplistic mindset that assumes, 'I am already a leader and hence what I am doing is leadership'. Instead, the leadership action the CEO takes has to stand scrutiny to this definition that we have given. And if indeed a CEO can do this—indirectly impact hundreds and thousands of people who are driving company performance through their daily actions—can you visualize the impact? That is when real magical and transformational changes in performance happen.

Another way of visualizing this is that many management actions are happening every day in the company, taken by managers across various layers. If each management action taken anywhere in the company improves a little bit because of the CEO's leadership, then can you imagine the positive impact that would have? In a way, my argument is that if you want that magic, that unique strength that drives performance, there is no other option but to practise the real leadership as we have defined it. The passive approach simply won't do. The majority of a leader's time can go in 'managing' actions, but an important minority time must be spent in leading actions and the impact of that minority time and those leading actions on both the leader's performance and the business's performance will be very high.

Transform from just managing to 'managing + leading'

Unfortunately, currently, even spending that minority time in leading actions is not happening in many cases. I often find that as people go up the ladder and move into so-called leader roles, they don't really effectively transition their time spent between managing and leading. Career growth is a gradual process and hence, there is a tendency to continue doing what we have done in the past. In the process, some very conscious transitions in work style and priorities that need to be made, don't get made. I find many senior people effectively doing only managing actions and not doing leading actions at all. Their primary focus is only on what they are directly involved in. Further, that simplification of 'what the leader does is called leadership' helps hide the problem. Hence, many people get lulled into the false complacency of thinking 'I am leading' and don't have the self-awareness to realize that they are only managing and not leading. I call these people 'visiting card leaders'. They are leaders because they have the title, not because they are actually leading. In the early stages of our careers, a large percentage of our performance is in our direct control in most cases. However, as we grow in our careers, the percentage of our performance within our control keeps coming down slowly. As it keeps coming down, it is obvious that you must proportionately keep increasing the amount of leading you have to do versus the managing. But this is like the parable of the frog in the water that is being slowly heated. The frog never jumps out because the temperature increase is slow and gradual. Similarly, the need for increasing the focus on leading actions is a gradual one and hence gets missed out while people continue primarily with managing actions.

This is the second transformation I want you to make, which is to consciously increase the time, energy and focus you give to deliberate leadership actions as you keep growing in seniority within the organization. A quick way of checking for yourself is to ask what percentage of your performance is in your direct control and what percentage is not. Once you arrive at this percentage—it need not be precise, it is more a judgement—then ask yourself whether you are doing enough to have some positive impact on that portion which is not in your control. Are you leading enough or have you not allotted enough actions towards leading? Sometimes, not allotting more time towards leadership actions can be a problem not just for seniors, but also for some junior roles where a large percentage of performance is dependent on what others do and is not in direct control of the role holder. For e.g., for an area sales manager in a consumer company, a significant part of their performance depends on the performance of the sales team, the distributor and even the distributor's employees. Similarly, in a large call centre, the performance of many call centre operators actually makes a difference to the mid-level manager's performance. Despite not traditionally being considered senior 'leadership' roles, such positions require a high number of leading actions, no matter where they fall in the hierarchy of the organizational structure.

Once I was invited by a very senior leader from a multinational bank to conduct a session on 'how to succeed in your career' for his team. And I landed up expecting the session to be like any other session I conduct—with around 100 people or so. When I landed up for this session, I was amazed, as it was in one of the largest ballrooms of one of the largest hotels and the place was packed to the rafters. It was the largest crowd I had ever addressed. I thoroughly enjoyed the session and the audience loved it too. It went on for longer than usual. At the end of it, when I was having a cup of tea with the senior leader who had invited me to conduct the session in the first place, I asked him why he had invited such a large number of people. His answer impressed me. I was able to identify him as someone who was aware of the need to impact the people who delivered performance. He said, and I quote, 'Mouli, there are over 500 people in my profit centre. I know that your talk will inspire these people to try hard and succeed in their careers; and if even 20 per cent of them achieve more, it is going to directly impact my performance and the performance of the profit centre that I manage.' Here is a great example of a leader, one who was self-aware that his managing actions simply wouldn't be enough, and that he had to find ways of indirectly impacting the 500 people who delivered performance. He was practising a leading action, by leveraging me as a resource to indirectly impact these people. He was someone who intuitively grasped the definition of leading as the 'art of impacting people where you are not directly involved'.

You might say I am nitpicking too much at the definition of leading and that I keep coming back to it again and again. That is for two reasons. The first is to reinforce a tangible definition which tells you what you need to work on and improve. This definition clearly says that to become good at leading, you have to continuously improve on the art of impacting people and their actions without being directly involved. If I lack a clear definition, there is ambiguity on what I need to work on, and considering the complexity of the subject that is leadership, that ambiguity can be very deep. Think of the last leadership programme you attended and ask yourself whether you were single-mindedly clear on what exactly were the actions you needed to take to improve your leadership. When I meet people who come back from leadership programmes, in most instances, I don't get a clear answer.

The second reason for a sharp definition is to help you focus. The subjects of leading and managing are vast and if you truly have to master everything about leadership, then you possibly need to read 1000 books and also practise all of that. Hence, my attempt in this book has been to prioritize a few things for you on the topic of leading and managing, making it manageable for you to work on and master them. And this definition of leadership is one such attempt at helping you choose and focus to work on something specific. While I am sure there are many other facets and definitions of leadership that are important, I personally feel this definition will cover the bulk of what most of us need on a daily basis in our lives. Hence, to become a great leader, my recommendation is to think single-mindedly about how to further improve in the art of impacting people and actions where you yourself are not involved directly.

How to lead?

This now brings us to the million-dollar question: how do I impact people with whom I am not directly involved? How do I perform these leading actions? As I alluded to in the initial chapters, there are two broad categories of actions you can take to lead, what I call **leading by doing** and **leading by being.** The next two chapters are going to cover this in reasonable detail. Readers of *Catalyst* may recall that I had set up an equation for leadership impact called the VML equation which went like this:

Leadership impact = (Position + Content) x Values.

It means that the extent of leadership impact you can create is a function of your **position**, your **content** and your **values** (the human being you are). In a given position, if you want to grow your leadership impact further, it means you must improve your content and your values. This broadly correlates with what I call leading by doing and leading by being. You can get a feel of it based on what's shown below.

Leadership = (Position + Content) x Values

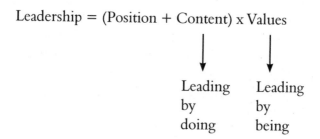

Leading   Leading
by   by
doing   being

A lot in this chapter has been written from the perspective of senior managers/leaders. However, as you know, I am a strong believer that everyone must lead and even the junior-most person must try and lead. Hence, I don't want the junior people to start thinking that leading is not for them. It is equally important for them. My favourite quote for junior people is, 'Start leading before you become a leader and you will become a leader faster than others.'

Good leadership is rare and that is something you can use to create an opportunity. The reason I say good leadership is rare is because most people are just managing, not leading. I say this with confidence because I often ask people a simple question, 'Have you thought about how to impact those people with whom you are not involved often?' And most people have a blank face for the answer. They have not even thought about how to impact where they are not involved, let alone actually do something about it. Think about whether you have ever thought about this; or would you also be among the many who have not even considered the subject of impacting people whom you are not involved with? If people have not even taken the time to consciously think about it, then I am guessing they obviously are not doing much to improve their ability to lead. Which is why I say with a lot of confidence that good leadership is rare; and that is why I am excited for you—because the opportunity is there for you to take. *There are such few people out there leading that if you start to lead, then you are going to be a super-duper success in your career and life.*

The starting point to good leading lies in two actions:

1. Stop using the words 'lead', 'leading' and 'leadership' loosely: use them only in the context of the definition we have agreed on, and you will find that this one change alone starts to significantly re-orient your thinking around leadership. When you stop loosely throwing around these words and start taking leadership seriously, then slowly, but surely, you will be forced to confront the actions you need to take to practise real leadership.

2. Ask yourself repeatedly, 'How can I improve my ability to impact those people with whom I am not directly involved often, and how can I improve my

ability to impact those management actions taken by others which happen out of my sight?'

Start doing these two things, reflect and leverage some of the techniques I give you in subsequent chapters, and you are going to be well on your way to becoming a real leader, and not just a leader on your visiting card title. Go forth and lead.

Chapter summary:

1. One of the great mistakes around leadership is the simplification that 'actions of leaders = leadership'. The first transformation we must make is to realize that simply because we are labelled as leaders, it does not imply that we are practising leadership. Instead, we have to start focusing on practising real leadership which is the art of impacting people and actions where you are not directly involved.

2. With seniority, the percentage of your performance in your direct control comes down and more and more of the performance is dependent on what others do. Many people don't realize this and continue primarily doing managerial actions even as they become senior. The second shift we have to consciously make is to increase the time and effort spent in leading as we become senior.

3. There are two broad ways of leading, *leading by doing* and *leading by being*. Both are important to become a good leader.

4. Good leaders are rare, most people are leaders on visiting cards because the companies call them leaders, but they actually don't lead in the way we have defined leading. And that is the opportunity for you, to be amongst the few who practise real leadership. To accelerate that:

    a. Stop using the words 'lead', 'leading' and 'leadership' loosely. Ask yourself whether the activity you are calling leadership stands up to our definition. You will start becoming aware of what real leadership is.

    b. Ask yourself every day, 'How do I improve my ability to impact those people with whom I am not directly involved, and how can I impact those management actions taken by others which happen out of my sight?'

9

Leadership by Doing

Most of you would have heard of the famous cathedral story somewhere or the other—I have seen it quoted in many leadership books and articles. The story goes something like this: Three people were building a wall. The first person, when asked what he was doing, said, 'I am building a wall.' The second said, 'I am building a perfect wall where each brick is perfectly aligned. There are no blemishes and the finish of the wall is excellent.' The third person said, 'I am building a cathedral.' All three were doing the same work, but all three were saying something different to themselves and to others about how they viewed their work.

Here is a situation for you to reflect on. Imagine yourself as the leader of the team that is building the cathedral. Based on your current leadership style, what answers do you think your team members would give when questioned about what they are doing? Would they view their tasks more transactionally and factually, as the first or second person did in the above analogy, or would they describe the greater purpose of their tasks, such as the third person did? The cathedral is just an analogy to help you think honestly about how you lead today, and whether the people you lead respond about what they do at work in a transactional way or from a higher sense of purpose. Are you able to help your team see the greater purpose of their work through your leadership? Write down a few points of your reflection about your own leadership style here:

1.

2.

The first question that may come to you is, 'Why is it important what they say? Does it really affect the output?' The answer is yes, it makes a difference—people who view their tasks at a higher-order level often have a greater degree of engagement and commitment to their work. They feel pride, take responsibility and most importantly, they almost always have a positive impact on others around them. Hence, it is important as a leader to get your people to think about their work at a higher-order level and not at a transactional level. The second question could be, 'How does one get them to speak of their work from a greater sense of purpose?' That is where leadership actions come in. A highly motivated employee might build a purposive narrative for themselves without any help, *but, for most people we lead, it becomes our job to help them articulate for themselves what is it that they do and how that can be meaningful.*

Now it might seem easier to define this purpose with something like a cathedral or a temple which already has a noble purpose, but what about the industries you and I work in—credit card companies, soap manufacturing, e-commerce, IT, etc.? It is not easy to look at commercial, practical organizations and find 'purpose' immediately. But if we try doing that, it creates value for our work in our own minds. Let me illustrate this with examples of companies I have worked with.

For example, in Asian Paints, the common purpose would be 'to sell paints', but a more purpose-driven narrative could be, 'We add beauty to homes that families enjoy living in'. If we look at Onida and TVs, the simple purpose is 'we sell televisions' while a way of defining it with a 'higher' purpose could be, 'We help add entertainment to people's lives'.

This came alive for me once in Cadbury. One day, when we were on a store visit, a girl walked in, opened the purple Cadbury fridge kept at the front of the store, took a bar of chocolate, paid for it, and walked away. The salesperson immediately said, 'That is good, a sale happened right in front of our eyes.' After a little bit of banter, I chipped in and said, 'That girl is going to sit down somewhere, enjoy the chocolate and have a few moments of happiness and delight soon. Or maybe she is going to give that chocolate to a friend who might be celebrating a birthday today and make the friend happy— that is what has happened just now.' Everyone looked at me and smiled. It was a spontaneous smile. I think I inadvertently defined a higher purpose to the sale.

Imagine if we tried to define the deeper purpose of our work along these lines on a regular basis—how much more would it motivate us as compared to just going about our daily work and its transactions/operations!

Now some of you, who are more practical and analytical, might say that this is starting to go into a warm, fuzzy area and has no real practical value. Fifteen years ago, I would have also possibly agreed with you and said, 'What is this warm, fuzzy mumbo-jumbo? This kind of stuff does not have a place in the real world.' But my own learning process, my evolution as a leader, has taught me otherwise and I no longer dismiss it as warm, fuzzy mumbo-jumbo. Of course, if we only talk about the more emotional purpose, and don't back it with enough real managerial actions and tangible leadership actions, then it certainly sounds hollow and perhaps even like we are actually fooling people. But, if you add this purpose-building to the many things you are already doing, then it certainly has an incremental value and that has been my learning over time.

So, according to me, one of the most important leadership actions for you to take is to help your people build a narrative for themselves on what is the work that they are doing, so as to get themselves to give meaning to that work, and in doing so, make them more engaged and more committed. This is the first outcome we want from *leading by doing*.

There is another very important outcome of 'leading by doing' and that is guiding people's actions even when you are not present.

So far, in this chapter, we have been exploring the first outcome of leading by doing, i.e., building the narrative. In the later part of the chapter, I shall spend time on the second outcome of guiding their actions as well. When you successfully achieve both these outcomes, then you are impacting people and actions even when you are not directly involved. The reason both these come under 'leading by doing' is because it takes deliberate leadership actions on your part to enable these to happen. They are not going to happen by themselves. They take some *doing* and your leading actions have to facilitate this. The strategy I have developed for you to be effective in achieving these two outcomes; to be effective in leading by doing, is what I call VISA.

VISA

VISA is an acronym for **V**ision, **I**nspiration, **S**trategic Clarity and **A**lignment. As a leader, if you are able to provide these four things to your team/employees, then you are going to achieve the twin objectives of helping them build a narrative for their work and guiding their actions when you are out of sight. Before I get into explaining each of these, I want to give you the visualization behind how I got to the acronym. It is not just convenient, but also a word that has deep meaning. We are all familiar with the word 'visa' which is the permission that you have to take to enter another country. It is stamped on your passport. Once you get the visa, you are free to fly, subject to the rules of the visa.

That is the visualization I want you to have. I want you to give a visa to the people you lead; give them the permission to fly freely, but with the confidence that you have handed them the rules of the visa too. You have given them a direction and boundary conditions by articulating the vision, by inspiring them, by giving them strategic clarity and by aligning them. Close your eyes and visualize this for a moment—you have given the people you lead the VISA to fly freely and are able to see them flying with a sense of purpose and energy. They are getting things done all by themselves without your guidance. Take a few minutes to visualize this. Close your eyes and imagine real people from among your employees flying, being happy, and getting things done. It will give you positive energy and a sense of motivation to do this. *That in essence is what great leadership is about—give people the direction, the inspiration and some boundary conditions and then let them fly*. And when people fly like that, they achieve remarkable stuff for you and your employees and they are happy doing it.

As we said before, leading by doing has to solve for two aspects:

1. Help people build a narrative for what they do at work.
2. Guide their actions when you are not present.

From VISA, typically V and I help us achieve the first outcome which is helping people build a narrative and meaning for what they do at work. S and A help achieve the second outcome of guiding their actions when you are not involved. This is a very broad correlation and, of course, there are some overlap areas, but it helps us build a picture of what V and I impact and what S and A impact.

Let us go outcome by outcome and explore what we can 'do' as leaders leveraging VISA to get to those outcomes.

Help people build a narrative and meaning around what they do at work

We started with the cathedral story, which, in a way, was about how people give themselves a narrative at work. That narrative they provide themselves with impacts their motivation, their engagement and the effort and commitment they put in. We also discussed some examples of similar narratives in the real world using paints, TVs, chocolates, etc. Most of those narratives were consumer-facing, i.e., how does what I do positively impact the consumer of the product/service I provide? The consumer/customer route is one source of building narratives, but there are other sources of building narratives too that you can use. One type could be social/ environmental aspects—how does the kind of work that people do impact society and the environment? It can be internal such as 'wanting to be THE business unit in the organization and always setting standards for others on financial performance'. The narrative that people give themselves for the work they do can be fashioned at any level and in any style. It does not have to be restricted to any one approach.

A powerful example of how people may derive a narrative from multiple sources is a noble profession like the army or any other defence force. At one level, a soldier has the narrative that, 'I fight for my country and its people.' At another, the same soldier may have a narrative that 'I fight for the pride and history of my regiment, my unit, and I will do my best to uphold the honour and tradition of my regiment.' At yet another level, a soldier may have a narrative relating to a specific mission: 'I have to be highly effective to complete this mission successfully.' And at another level that soldier can simply have the narrative, 'I am fighting for the four others who are fighting with me. I have to do well for their sake and our collective sake.' This is a great example of how people can build motivating narratives from multiple sources. It is our job as leaders to provide them the raw material for fashioning the narrative, provide them the vision and the inspiration—the V and I of VISA—for them to fashion these narratives for the work they do.

V for Vision

Vision is one of those complex words that is challenging to define and understand. Often, along with vision, we see a set of related words—'mission' and 'purpose'— which form a triad. So, when I refer to vision in VISA, I refer to the triad in a collective way. It does seem like splitting hairs, but let me try and use a healthcare company example to give you a feel of what these words broadly stand for.

Let us visualize a healthcare company in cancer care. The company's vision is a statement of the direction that they are headed in. For e.g., this company could have a vision that says, 'We want to democratize cancer care.' The mission is broadly about the process to actually get to the vision—the means; and this company could have a mission like, 'We will make cancer care affordable and accessible.' Purpose is about the why behind wanting to achieve this vision; and this company could have a purpose like 'We want to save lives.' Put together, it reads, 'We want to democratize cancer care by making it affordable and accessible which will help save lives.' I hope this gives you a sense of clarity around the three words and how they are different and yet integrated with each other. Having said that, the macro objective of this exercise is to give the people we lead a broad picture, a vision. I don't want to spend time hair-splitting between the words as long as we achieve the macro objective.

When we think vision, we can think of it at two levels. The companies that we work in, typically, already tend to have a defined vision, mission, and purpose. The second level is the unit you head and the people you lead. It could be a call centre, a city or a state, a function, a profit centre, etc. In providing vision to your employees, you can operate at both levels as explained below.

Leverage your company vision, mission, purpose

Starting with the company vision, the question is, how can you, as a leader, use this vision to engage and motivate your team and help them build a narrative for what they do. Often, company vision, mission, purpose, etc., are on paper and available on websites, but they rarely make a difference to the average team member. That is because seldom do we, the leaders, bring them to life in a meaningful way. We keep waiting for corporate communications or someone else from the top to do that.

So, the simplest thing in *leadership by doing* is to bring the company vision alive for the team you lead.

We can do this by:

1. Simply talking about it in our sessions; encouraging people to talk about it, asking them what meaning they get out of it, etc. Creating a conversation at a reasonable frequency about what is on paper, putting it on a slide and discussing it in a meeting—these enable our teams to derive narratives out of the company-level vision.

2. There could be other techniques that you could adopt too. For e.g., when I was a marketer at Asian Paints, I have gone on consumer home visits. The expressions of delight and joy on the faces of family members when they see their newly painted home would always bring a smile to my face. If I were still in Asian Paints and the company vision was, 'We make beautiful homes that families can enjoy living in,' I would want to capture on video several such moments of consumer delight, the joy on their faces, the words they use to describe their feelings and then show it to people in various company departments such as accounts, and in the factories. I'd say, 'This is the impact your work creates. You are not just in accounts and paying vendors; you are helping create this joy; you are not in a factory just producing a can of paint, you are helping create this joy.'

In summary, your company vision can be a powerful way of helping your team build a narrative. However, it won't happen by itself and that is why it comes under leadership by doing; you have to do something to bring it alive. The more creative and passionate you are in bringing it alive, the more the impact on the people you lead.

Leverage/Create a unit-level vision

The second level is at your unit or team level or however you would like to define the boundaries of the people you lead. You could be a factory head, a city/state head, you could be heading a vertical within a function, or you could be running customer service. You can define your unit in any way based on what your actual reality is. Many a time, I find that apart from the company-level vision, having a unit-level vision helps people build even stronger and more purposeful narratives on what they do at work. For e.g., if you head a category/vertical in an e-commerce company, you could have a vision of, 'We will be the vertical that has the highest customer satisfaction amongst all verticals in our company.' Typically, a unit-level vision would lack the grandiose feel of a company-level vision, but it makes up for that by being more tangible and relevant to the team, thus making it into something they can act upon at work every day. Hence, I am a strong proponent of you building a unit-level vision for the teams you lead. However, the same caveats do apply. Simply doing this exercise once and then leaving it to remain on paper is really not useful. But if you bring it alive often; if you integrate it in all your communication to the team and in your ways of working, then it can really engage your team and help them build their narrative.

I for Inspiration

The next important thing in VISA is inspiring people. Even before we start, let us understand the word 'inspire'. This is another word in the leadership dictionary which can mean a lot and can be used in several contexts—some right and many, not-so-right. I want you to spend a minute thinking about this word; ask yourself its meaning, and visualize what will happen when you inspire your team and write down a few points here:

1.

2.

I also spent quite a few years using this word without truly understanding its meaning. I have also often been called an 'inspiring leader' without possibly understanding what it meant. However, when I sat down to write this chapter, I decided I needed to have a clear articulation for this word. So, after some star gazing and thinking, here is the conclusion I arrived at:

What happens when you get inspired? *When you get inspired, you effectively reset your standards to a higher level; you start to think of doing things which otherwise you might not have considered, you start to now think that something is possible that you earlier considered difficult or impossible, etc.* So, in a small town where admissions to prestigious academic institutions like IITs are considered out of reach, the first kid who gets through suddenly inspires everyone else in that small town to believe that it is possible. As a corporate person, listening to para-athlete and Olympian Deepa Malik during a leadership session organized by Pidilite was inspiring; here was a person who, despite being paralysed waist down, decided she would do something with her life and trained herself in Olympic sports to become one of the most celebrated Indian Olympians. It inspired me and made me think nothing is impossible. Mind over matter is all you need to commit to something difficult. So, when you set out to inspire your team, that is what you are aiming for—you are aiming to reset their standards; trying to change their passion and energy levels, change what they believed was possible, make them think that new things are possible, etc. That is the objective of inspiration and that is when you can be called an 'inspiring leader'.

Which then brings us to the 'how' of inspiration: what can you, as a leader, *do* to inspire?

The first and the most important thing is to always lead with the bigger picture. Just as I was writing this chapter, I read a tweet from Dr N.S. Rajan, ex-CHRO, Tata Sons, one of the most illustrious of HR professionals and leaders. The tweet read and I quote, 'When folks in an organization don't understand the bigger picture, it makes them feel like small players.' My own belief in this is very strong and my own model of inspiring people has strongly rested on communicating the bigger picture. Never tell people just what they are supposed to do, tell them 'why', show them the bigger picture, show them how what they do makes a difference to the bigger picture. When people see that what they do makes a difference, it inspires them, changes their passion and energy levels.

This requires some effort, preparation and change from us as leaders. Often, our discussions and communication quickly degenerate to the task at hand—to what needs to be done—and very little time is spent on the 'why', the bigger picture. As a leader, you have to make a conscious effort to lead with the bigger picture and the 'why', if you want to be inspiring.

The second thing you can do to inspire is to lead with possibilities, not challenges. In any initiative, there are possibilities/opportunities that the successful execution of the initiative would result in and there are challenges in execution. As a leader, where does your natural instinct lie? What do you lead with? Again, my bias has been to paint the picture of possibilities, bring the opportunity alive, make people realize that it is worth putting effort into, and worth taking on the obstacles and only then would I come to the challenges of doing it. My teams always used to joke with me, 'If Mouli were to be believed, then the Indian market size would be three times the current size', and we would share a laugh. Possibilities are not about foolish optimism though; they are about being able to visualize what you might be able to achieve if you do a perfect job of something before starting to deal with the challenges. Seeing possibilities, seeing opportunities, inspires people and makes them reset their standards.

The third thing you have to do to inspire is to get the balance right between discussing success stories and problems. Imagine you are having a day-long meeting where you are chairing and others are presenting. The way you choose to set the agenda will define how many success stories get presented or whether more time is spent discussing the issues that need to be solved. Nothing inspires people more than success stories showcasing what is possible and that it can be done. In this case, you don't need to even speak a word, you just need to get the balance of the agenda right. We have all been part of meetings held by our bosses and leaders where the discussions are only about problems. After a point, it becomes very grim and when we come out of the meeting, we are convinced that things are too difficult and nothing that we discussed in the meeting is actually possible. *Think of such a meeting you attended. Don't let your meetings become like that.* As a leader, even in the most challenging of situations, keep a healthy balance between success stories and problems to be solved. It is the success stories that inspire people and give them the energy to tackle problems. If we only discuss problems, we might have answers, but not the passion and energy required behind those answers.

The fourth thing you can do to inspire people is to get more external speakers to talk to your teams. Every time I have sat in a session involving an external speaker, I am almost always inspired. When you look back, you will also find that you have had a similar experience. Some external speakers can really inspire. They are highly credible because they are neutral and don't have a company agenda. I must admit, I myself did not use this strategy enough to inspire my teams, but in retrospect, I am convinced that this is a powerful strategy. Set a rhythm—maybe once a month—and bring in external speakers for keynotes. You will find that it really inspires people.

A great example of how inspired teams consistently produce magic is Fevicol's advertising. People always ask how it is possible for a brand, over many decades, to produce such fantastic advertising consistently, as it does not happen often in the marketing world. While one could offer many marketing theories as explanations, I do think it finally comes down to the fact that the people involved in Fevicol's advertising are an inspired lot—inspired by past and present success stories, by possibilities, and by the Pidilite leadership team's belief in them. This inspired team keeps resetting the standards and raising the bar for the future and so, the saga continues. Inspire the people you lead consistently and then prepare to get amazed by the resultant magic.

V and I are, therefore, important toolkits of 'leading by doing' to enable the people you lead to give themselves a positive narrative and meaning to their work—to get inspired. This gets you the engagement and commitment of your teams and gets the passion, the energy and the hearts of your teams into play. Let's now move on to the second outcome of leading by doing.

Guiding actions of others when you are not present

Early in my career, as a young sales manager in Asian Paints, the one thing that every single salesperson knew was that under no circumstances would we do anything unethical to drive sales. It could be the month end, there could be severe target pressures, but not one person would push stock that would result in an unhealthy sale, or do something else unhealthy with policy implementation, etc. When I was in Asian Paints, it seemed so easy and so obvious. It was only when I started working elsewhere that I realized how tough it was to create that culture and discipline where not even one salesperson amongst the hundreds that a company has, does anything unhealthy to achieve a target at the end of the month.

What were the benefits of this? One was credibility with customers—we always did exactly what we said we would. It was not one thing on paper and another thing in practice. The other advantage was that no problems—typical of unethical/underhanded actions—arose. When something unhealthy is done, it may create a short-term benefit, but soon results in a mess of problems taking a lot of your managerial effort to clean up. In some of the other companies I worked in, a lot of my time and attention went in cleaning up messes, while in Asian Paints, because everyone's actions were consistent, seldom did I spend time cleaning up. One of the important benefits of leading by doing is that the leading time spent in guiding the actions of others is often much lower than the managerial time you would have otherwise spent solving problems later on. *I always say, 'One good leading action can save a hundred managerial actions afterwards.'*

In a sense, the actions of every single salesperson at Asian Paints were guided by the strategy and philosophy of the leaders of the company, despite there being no direct enforcement of this strategy on a regular basis. Every individual, by themselves, was choosing to act in the right way, despite there being no oversight from leaders. The leaders had worked over a long time to instil this strategy and philosophy. This is, to me, a classic example of guiding actions of others when you are not there.

We defined leading as the art of impacting others when you are not directly involved. There is one other articulation of leading that I like which is worth mentioning in this context—**Leading is the art of influencing the managerial actions of others which they take in your absence or without your involvement.** As a leader, if you influence many of the managerial actions that others take when you are not around, then you are having greater impact. The means to doing that is providing 'strategic clarity' and building 'alignment'—the S and A of VISA.

S for Strategic clarity

Once, I worked in a business with a high market share. However, the market itself was not large and had a lot of scope for growth compared to other similar markets in the world. Hence, the bulk of our effort, time and resources was to be invested on growing the market and not on gaining market share. This is an example of strategic clarity; all the people I led were clear that the priority was market growth, not market share. This clarity made sure that when they were making plans, conceptualizing initiatives, thinking of new product and service ideas—all of that went towards growing the market. This strategic clarity was guiding their actions.

Sometimes, to provide strategic clarity, leaders end up emailing large strategy decks to their teams—a few hundred pages of strategy. I definitely recommend that such decks be shared transparently, but that is not going to provide the strategic clarity we are talking about. We want to guide people's actions when we are not there.

That requires simpler and easier communication of strategy, not a large deck.

To guide people's actions, you must communicate the following:

1. Clarity on the big objectives: What are we chasing? For e.g., the market growth versus market share example.
2. Clarity on boundary conditions:
   a. What's within our boundary and what lies outside?
   b. What are our non-negotiables?

Do an exercise—call ten random people from various levels in your team and ask them to sit for half an hour and write the answers to the above questions without you saying anything. When you see the answers, you might get amazed at how different they are and how different people have a completely different understanding of both the big objectives and the major boundaries. This will convince you of the need to be more effective in developing strategic clarity among the people you lead.

If you can ingrain the big objectives and the boundary conditions in your team, you will have gone a long way in creating strategic clarity. *The game lies in not just defining the strategy at the top management levels, but in communicating the same and making sure it gets understood and internalized by your teams.* A lot of strategy gets created, but seldom does it get communicated; in which case, it is not useful because that strategy is not guiding the actions of many people in the organization. The only strategy that really gets implemented is the strategy that is communicated, understood and internalized by the people you lead. A boss of mine used to say that company strategy must be simple enough that even the watchman and the receptionist are aware of it. You don't have to take this literally, but you have got the drift of what he meant. So, it is important to really spend a lot of time communicating the strategy, discussing it, and addressing any questions to the contrary. And this should not be done just once, but repeatedly at some frequency—my judgement is at least twice a year.

Apple is an example of a company where, even as an outsider, I can sense exceptional strategic clarity. The big objective seems to be clear—we are in the high-end personal devices market and, in most cases, we will create a market where none exists. The boundary conditions also seem crystal clear—the user interface must be simple and easy; the packaging must be so elegant and flawless that a consumer feels a great deal of pride when buying an Apple product, the design must be drool-worthy yet minimalistic and not flashy, the pricing and positioning will always be premium. I could go on and on. But you can really see the power of this strategic clarity. It's a great example of how an entire organization's actions can be guided, and people can be allowed to fly when you have such clarity.

There are two benefits to having strategic clarity. The first is that people stay focused on tasks that contribute to the strategy, and don't waste time on unrelated activities, despite minimal supervision. The second is that people are far more willing to accept and operate within boundary conditions, if they are communicated in advance. When they have to work without clarity on what's allowed and what isn't, they can easily get frustrated at being told that things can't be done a certain way. You can avoid this frustration by ensuring everyone is on the same page before they start.

In fact, the best way to judge whether you have provided strategic clarity to your teams is by seeing how often you agree with the work done by your team and how often you have to disagree and say no. When your team brings you the work they have done, and you find that you often agree with the basic premise, then strategic clarity is high. Of course, you will add value to what they have done, provide suggestions and improvement ideas, but at the core, you are aligned. If the opposite is happening where you have fundamental disagreements with your team and often say 'no' to what they propose, even after they have done a lot of work, then there is a problem. *In your mind, you might think that the problem is the capability/competence of the team, but the real underlying problem is likely to be that you have not provided strategic clarity.* Learn to recognize that symptom and work on providing strategic clarity. You will be surprised at how quickly the 'incompetent' team becomes competent.

A for Alignment

Many of you would have heard of the popular boat race during Onam in Kerala or the famous annual boat race between Oxford and Cambridge in the UK. In any boat race, three things have to happen for the teams to do well:

1. The boat has to point in the right direction.
2. Each rower has to row in the same direction; no one should be rowing in the opposite direction.

3. All the rowers need to row to the same rhythm. All the oars have to enter the water at the same time and leave the water at the same time.

Now, all this seems obvious and easy to do for a boat race—that is the whole point, after all. But shouldn't this be as obvious and as easy to do for the companies you and I work in? In companies, as I have experienced it, point one does happen often—the companies have the right idea of where to head. But points two and three, which is having *everyone* rowing in the same direction and to the same rhythm, are often big problems. In my career, there have been several times where I have felt that I am fighting many more battles within my company than outside in the market and that is because of points two and three. Not everyone would be rowing in the same direction—someone with whom I would have to partner to make something happen would be rowing in another direction and a lot of my energy and time would go in convincing that person to change direction, or in rowing harder to neutralize the force they are exerting in the opposite direction. The same thing goes for rowing rhythm—you may be working on an important initiative and the person you have to work with in some other part of the company might be working on something else and will come to your initiative after a month. We have all experienced these things and faced enormous frustrations with them. Often, our anger and frustration are aimed at the other person, but that person rarely has poor intent. They are not intentionally rowing in the opposite direction to make your life difficult or operating to a different rhythm and delaying your initiative because they don't like your face. It simply happens because the people who are leading us have done a poor job of building alignment amongst us. You and the other person are not aligned on the same priorities. *It is a leadership and alignment problem, not an individual problem, much as it might feel like that at that point of time.* The exact same thing could be happening in your teams; people could be getting frustrated with internal battles because you have not aligned them.

One of your most important roles when leading is to ensure that your teams are not working at cross purposes, but in an aligned manner. The things that you have to align are the same as in the boat race.

1. Is the boat pointing in the right direction? Is everyone aligned to the vision and the direction? Do they have a common, collective sense of where we are heading?
2. Getting everyone rowing in the same direction. This is about aligning priorities—if everyone has the same priorities, then they will row in the same direction.
3. Getting everyone to row to the same rhythm. This goes beyond aligned priorities to everyone having the same aligned timelines for priorities.

If you are able to align the teams you lead on the above three aspects, then you will find that your organization is functioning like a well-oiled machine and delivers great output. I know that it is not an easy process, and I have encountered many challenges and insights during my career:

1. Typically, pointing the boat in the right direction is relatively easy if you give people the right vision and they get it.

2. The challenge in point two—getting everyone to row in the same direction is that simply having everyone say 'yes' when you spell out the priorities doesn't mean that the alignment is done. Seldom do they say 'no' to a priority spelt out by a leader. But the problem is that they also create their own priorities over and above your list and hence, effectively, the desired prioritization does not happen. There are two possible mitigations to this: a) you get a positive time commitment saying they will spend, say, 60 per cent of their time on the priorities defined by the leader (you) or b) you have a way of reducing the number of other priorities they generate. For example, as a leader, if you want to set the priority as 'customer engagement', you will have to converse extensively with your team members to understand what other priorities they have that would make them unwilling to commit that much time to customer engagement. Then, you can further shortlist the ones that can be ignored, and agree on shelving those permanently or to come back to them later.

3. The challenge in point three of getting people to row at the same rhythm is this: people like working on initiatives they are leading but could have lower enthusiasm for initiatives others are leading to which they are just contributors. This causes the rhythm problem; everyone is working on their pet initiatives and the whole team is not acting in unison, at the same

time, on key initiatives. To mitigate this, a good way is to hold the whole team accountable for the initiative, and not just the leader. So, when things go well, you should distribute the credit to the whole team. If you want, in private and in annual appraisals, you can be more discerning on who should get the credit or the debit, but largely, with the team involved in the initiative, make it a matter of collective responsibility.

One of the most powerful examples of a well-executed S and A of VISA was when I was in Cadbury/Mondelez and Anand Kripalu was the MD. Between Anand and I, we formulated eight strategic priorities for the business and widely communicated them so that everyone knew these were the only eight things that the company would focus on. But it did not stop there; they were built into scorecards. The first one hour of any leadership team meeting was spent discussing the eight strategic priorities. Anand, in every town hall, would communicate transparently on the eight priorities to the entire company. They were made a part of annual goal sheets and KRAs of people. And most important was the consistency that Anand maintained; his belief was that such priorities take time to percolate and get ingrained, and we must not change them often. This combination of sharp strategic clarity coupled with a high degree of alignment within the company created a really strong performance for the organization.

So that is VISA, your toolkit for 'leading by doing'. If you can effectively help your people build a narrative and meaning for what they do at work by painting a 'Vision' and 'Inspiring' them, and if you can guide the actions that they will perform when you are out of sight, by providing 'Strategic clarity' and driving 'Alignment', then you are going to be a very effective leader and your team would be a super-performing, highly effective team. Close your eyes and visualize this: you have given the team the VISA and they are all flying now, highly charged; doing great things, being happy, all within the guidelines and the boundaries set by your VISA. That is what your leadership is capable of—creating such a team. Go forth and make people fly!

Chapter summary:

1. Leading by doing has to solve for two aspects:

    a. Help people build a narrative and meaning for what they do at work.
    b. Guide their actions when you are not present.

2. To be able to do that, you must use the toolkit of VISA, which is, providing your people with Vision, Inspiration, Strategic clarity and Alignment. Typically, V and I help people build a narrative for their work, while S and A guide their actions.

3. You can provide vision by doing two things:

    a. Leverage your company-level vision, mission, purpose, etc. Create discussion forums in your teams for this and let them discover meaning from these.
    b. Create a unit/team level vision which also makes it more tangible and actionable on a daily basis in their jobs.

4. Inspiring is about raising people's standards, their passion and commitment and, making them believe that more is possible, new is possible, etc. To inspire, you should do three things:

    a. Always lead with the bigger picture—'why' are we doing something. When people get the bigger picture, they are themselves inspired to put together the nuts and bolts and even more.
    b. Lead with the possibilities—the opportunity of doing something rather than the problems of doing something. If people can smell the possibility/opportunity, then they get the energy to solve problems.
    c. Always keep a healthy balance of success stories and problems to be solved in your meetings. Meetings focused only on problems not only create negative energy, but, more often than not, convince people that the problems are too grim and possibly not solvable.
    d. Leverage external speakers, industry experts, etc. to talk to your teams.

5. Strategic clarity is about providing clear direction and boundary conditions to enable people to act by themselves.

    a. Provide clarity on the big objectives—what are we chasing and what are we not chasing. Also, set boundary conditions—what's in and what's out as well as key 'non-negotiables' in how we do things.

b. Having a strategy is not enough, there has to be a lot of focus on communicating it till it is well understood by the team.

c. Strategic clarity helps people focus on what matters and not get frustrated by doing a lot of work on something only to be told 'no' at the last stage. The single biggest symptom of poor strategic clarity is the number of times you have to say 'no' to your teams. If that is high, then the problem lies in the strategic clarity you provided.

6. Alignment is about aligning both priorities and their timelines. The purpose of alignment is to ensure that the entire organization works in unison on key priorities and to the same rhythm. Alignment often breaks down, not because people say 'no' to identified priorities, but because they add several other priorities of their own beyond that.

10

Leadership by Being

'Who you are is how you lead'

I want to set you a challenge and get you to spend some time thinking about how you would overcome it. Your challenge is this—get one person to resign from their current job. Assume that person is middle-aged and economically not well off. You have to make them leave their job without really knowing for sure what they will do next. There might be another job available, there might not be. You have to accomplish this challenge under the following conditions:

1. The person is a complete stranger; never in the past have you personally ever met or spoken or had any connection with that person.
2. You can have no communication with them in any form, written or oral or audio-visual.

Think for five minutes on how you would solve this problem within the conditions I have set. This is not a trick question. We are in a leadership learning process so think with that lens and do not try to find a solution by finding some loophole in the conditions. Write down your reflections below:

1.

2.

So, were you able to come up with a strategy to achieve this objective? Did it seem an impossible challenge? It does feel like getting someone—who is economically not very well off—to give up a job without knowing what's next is already difficult even under normal circumstances. To do that to a stranger without being able to communicate with them in any way seems impossible. Does it not?

Well, there was one man who managed to do it. And it wasn't just one person who gave up their job, but thousands who gave up their jobs because he asked them to. His name was Mohandas Karamchand Gandhi and he was possibly one of the all-time greats in India from a pure leadership perspective, leave alone his contribution to the nation. The impossible conditions I set for you were actually a representation of the real challenges he faced and how his leadership overcame them. Let me explain below how the conditions I set you were actually real issues he faced in his leadership.

Gandhiji was leading in an era when literacy was low. It is estimated that literacy in India was around 5 per cent in the 1920s and around 7–8 per cent in the 1930s. Hence, it meant that most Indians could not read and had most certainly never read anything that Gandhiji had written. They wouldn't even have read anything that newspapers wrote about him. Radio penetration in India was close to non-existent during that era. Bombay and Calcutta radio stations were set up only in 1927, and barely 3000 people are estimated to have owned a radio at that time. The Delhi station was set up even later, in 1936. So, it is also fair to assume that Gandhiji could not communicate with the Indian masses through radio. There was no TV and no other mass mode through which people could be reached. Basically, Gandhiji did not have any large-impact communication tools to engage and influence people. The only people who ever saw Gandhiji or heard his views and philosophies were those who attended a public meeting of his at some point of time. My guess is that this number would be less than 1 per cent of the total population of 272 million at that time. So, here's the situation: here was a massive population that had never met the man; never heard him speak, never read anything he wrote or never even saw him in person or on TV/film. Yet, that man was able to make people give up their government jobs in a civil disobedience movement; that man was able to get people to throw their imported clothes into a bonfire despite moderate economic means and, that man was able to get people to practise non-violence even when they themselves were hit violently at times. How do you think that does as far as leadership impact goes? How does that stand up to our definition of leading—the art of impacting people without any direct involvement?

Breathtaking, exemplary, stunning—those are the words that come to my mind when I assess him from a purely leadership lens. Leaving aside our individual views about his politics and ideologies, it would be hard for anyone to deny that this man was an extraordinary leader, possibly one of a kind who could impact a population of 272 million without speaking to them or them having read him or about him and without seeing him. The question is why was he able to do it—what gave his leadership that impact?

The answer lies in 'leading by being'. He was able to have that leadership impact because of the human being he was and how he lived his life on a daily basis. Tales of how he lived are legendary—the frugality, simplicity, and the humility to clean one's own toilet. His integrity and honesty were well-known. All told, his 'being', the human he was and the way he lived his life made 272 million Indians trust him despite never having had any contact with him. They placed their trust in who he was, and it was this trust that allowed him to mobilize the population for extraordinary causes, whenever required.

Gandhiji could not have done this on the first day he started. 'Leading by being' is like a bank account. Unless you deposit things like good values, behaviours and your way of life into this account on a continuous basis, you cannot withdraw from it. But once you have deposited enough and earned the trust of people, then the impact is extraordinary. If someone else gave a similar call asking for people to give up their jobs with the same logic and articulation as Gandhiji did, it would not have succeeded unless that person had built a deposit as well as Gandhiji had built by his 'being'. It was less about 'what' was being said and more about 'who' said it. That is the ultimate level of leadership, where people follow you for 'who' you are and not based on logically evaluating everything you say. If you set high standards of 'leading by being' then one day, people will follow you for **who you are**, rather than for your strategies and business actions. Those will just be secondary reasons for creating leadership impact.

So how does one build 'leadership by being'? The answer is simple—it depends on you 'being' the right kind of person all the time. As a corporate person and leader, people in your company are always observing you in whatever you do. They don't just hear what you say. They see your behaviour, they observe and impute your values and assess you as a role model when it comes to challenging and difficult issues. A mentor of mine used to say, 'Leading is the act of being on the stage all the time. You are never off it and the lights are always on you.' That is the truth. As you seek to lead, you will be observed all the time and how you are at all those times builds up your bank deposit for 'leading by being'. Now, any actor can get on the stage and act. When they get off, they will be a different person. But we are not trained actors, and we can't say we will act like one person in a business situation and then we will be someone else once we are not in any official situation. *You can't act like a good human being; you have to be a good human being.* The real you will be seen by everyone; that personality cannot be hidden or stage-managed. Hence, leading by being and wanting to become a great leader does require us to be or become great human beings.

There are many aspects to 'being'—there are many aspects of you that others will notice, and while a lot of that is important, in the spirit of this book making things practical and actionable for you, I have prioritized and made three choices regarding things that people will observe in you all the time.

1. Values
2. Behaviours towards people
3. Role modelling on difficult and complex issues

Values

Earlier in Chapter 8, I had introduced the VML equation for leadership impact which I had initially formulated in my first book, *Catalyst*.

The equation looks like this:

Leadership impact = (Position + Content) x Values

Leadership impact is the impact and influence you are able to have on a wide mass of people in your company, and often, even outside your company. As per the VML equation, this leadership impact of yours is driven by your position, your content, and your values.

1. Position—The higher your position, your title in the company, the greater the opportunity for leadership impact and vice versa.
2. Content—It is driven by what you say, what decisions you make, the strategies you have, etc.

The better your content, the higher the leadership impact and vice versa.

3. Values—The better the values you have, the greater the leadership impact you can build and the poorer the values, the worse is the leadership impact.

While all these three variables influence leadership impact, the equation was constructed the way it was to show you that not all three of these variables are equal in their contribution to your leadership impact. 'VML' stands for '**V**alue **M**ultiplies **L**eadership', and that is the construct of the equation. *Values* have a huge impact on leadership and are multiplicative, not additive. For the same position and content, two different people can have varying levels of leadership impact simply based on their values, and we have all experienced that. For those who are interested in how this equation was derived with the logical argument, I would urge you to read *Catalyst*. Here, I want to focus more on the application, usage, and implications of this equation for 'leading by being'.

Why do values have such a high influence on the leadership you can generate? At its core, leading is about getting a set of people to follow you on a journey, move in the direction indicated by you, take actions as visualized and communicated by you and so on. People follow based on their judgement of two factors: (i) 'what' is being said or asked and (ii) 'who' is saying or asking. You may be able to influence people whom you are in close touch with and have a fair degree of involvement with through the 'what'. There is sufficient trust built through interactions and time, and so, they can be convinced by the content and logic of the argument, and may even participate in building it. But if we look at a wider mass of people, and as we look at our definition of leading—leading is the art of impacting people where you are not directly involved—the 'who' becomes more important. It is obviously difficult to find the time and the opportunities to convince such a wide mass by explaining the 'what' to them, and the interaction opportunities are few and far between. Because of this, the repeated iterations of the 'what' that are required to build conviction are difficult to achieve. The Gandhiji example is a great proof of this. The more you want to impact people further away from you, the more 'who' says it becomes important. This is because, in your company, someone who is far away from you and meets you occasionally, will follow you on the journey you are wanting them to pursue with you only if they believe and trust in you. And this belief and trust is created by values, which define 'who' you are as a person. This is why I have elevated the role of 'who' over 'what' and the role of values over position and content.

If you see the depiction of the VML equation again (shown below), you can see the connection between the 'what', the 'who' and the equation. Always remember, leadership impact is a function of 'what' is being asked or said and 'who' is asking or saying it. If you want to grow the relative power of the 'who' in leadership impact, then values are important, *leadership by being* is important.

Leadership impact = (Position + Content) x Values

What   Who

Assuming you want to create a values-based leadership impact and want to grow the power of 'who', then the next automatic question is how one should approach it. I think there are two necessary conditions.

1. You should be reasonably high in all values.
2. There should be a few values where you should be at what I call the 'lodestar' standard, in which you are head and shoulders above anyone else, values that, in a way, define you.

There are many values—if I take a count based on different websites, it ranges from 100–250. I do think it is reasonably important to be good in all of them to become a good leader. It might seem intimidating that you have to be good in so many values, but my sense is that if you focus on being a good 'human being', then there is a fair chance that you will be fairly high in most values. I don't want to sermonize here on the importance of being, high in most values or the importance of being a good human being to be a good leader. I am sure you already get it.

Instead, I want to focus here on what can differentiate you, your lodestar values. Most great leaders became great because they truly had a few lodestar values. And that is the approach I recommend you take to become a great leader—identify a few values core to you and then achieve lodestar standards in them, which means you are head and shoulders above anyone else in your practice of that value. Let us take a few examples again of famous leaders to understand the concept of lodestar values. Going back to Gandhiji, my judgement as an observer is that his lodestar values were *integrity/honesty* and *simplicity/ frugality*. I believe that in these values, Gandhiji was at a lodestar level where very few could come up to his level. Ultimately, it is these values that earned him the trust of the population. His integrity meant that people believed he was doing the right thing and his simplicity/ frugality meant that people believed that he was not doing anything for his own selfish reasons such as to gain wealth, etc. While Gandhiji was surely good in most values, these two lodestar values of his helped him build the trust, and hence the leadership impact required. Let us take another example of Mother Teresa and her work with the Missionaries of Charity. My belief is her lodestar values were *compassion* and *empathy*. These lodestar values made her feel for every sick person and destitute person and these values helped her attract volunteers, funding support and co-workers who were committed to the same cause. This resulted in the creation of a large social service organization called the Missionaries of Charity. I hope these examples help you understand the concept of a few lodestar values. While being good in most values, if you become exceptional and reach lodestar levels in a few, that can create extraordinary leadership impact for you. I must put a disclaimer here that my comments on these leaders are purely as an observer and not based on any deep research of their values.

Choosing your lodestar values

This brings us to the next important question: how should we choose our lodestar values? I believe there is a two-step process in making this choice. The first step is about identifying your core values, and the general understanding of this is that there are a few values that you hold very dearly, which define you. If you Google how to find your core values, you will find umpteen websites, tools and literature that will help you. Please do take the effort to discover your core values, as it is difficult to build leadership impact without the awareness of that basic starting point.

Once you have arrived at a list of your core values, you can use these indicator questions to validate if each of these values is indeed core to you:

1. Do you feel that the value defines you in some ways, and is an important part of the nature of the human being you are?
2. Do you practise that value at a high standard, an indicator of that would be when you consciously take challenges, discomfort and some amount of pain (need not be just physical) to practise that value?
3. Have you selected that value because it is truly core to you or did you select it because you think it will look impressive in front of others?

Once you asked these basic sense check questions, you can finalize the list of your core values. Ideally, this list should not be longer than five to seven values.

The second step is about choosing a couple of lodestar values from the list of your core values. This should be done based on which of these core values could have the greatest leadership impact in the culture and context that you are in. There are different contexts—it could be a business and entrepreneurial context, or sports, creative and artistic fields, political and social spaces and so on. I do believe that different values have different potential for creating leadership impact depending on the context. For e.g., frugality/ simple living might be a high-impact value in a socio-political leadership context but it may not have the same impact in a sports leadership context. So please choose those lodestar values which have the highest potential for leadership impact in your context.

Often, in my workshops, given that most of them happen in corporates and entrepreneurial firms (I am yet to be invited by a film company or a sporting team to do a leadership workshop), I get asked by participants what I think are the values with possibly the highest potential for impact in the business context. Once, I sat down and from a website which listed a total of 200 values, chose the following twenty as the ones which I think have high potential as lodestar values in the corporate context.

These are: Accountability, adaptability, ambition, commitment, consistency, creativity, cooperation, decisiveness, determination/resilience, excellence, fairness, honesty, humility, optimism, openness, responsible, rigour, stewardship, teamwork and transparency.

Having said that, as I wrote above, this is a deeply personal process, and I do not recommend that you get constrained by my list. Please follow the process: in step one, identify your list of five–seven core values and then from that, in step two, choose two of them as your lodestar values based on the context you are in and if those two values are not on my list, it does not matter.

Building the muscle for the lodestar level

Now, we reach the core issue we all need to solve for before we can say we are leading by being. Just because we have identified what our lodestar values are does not mean we are practising it to lodestar standards, i.e., head and shoulders above the level that most others are practising that value at. At this stage, we have only identified them, and the journey to start practising them at lodestar standards has just begun. When we want to get fitter, we join the gym or do exercises; when we want to learn a new software, we read a book or take an online class, but when it comes to values, we somehow think it is natural and there is nothing that we have to do to improve on it. But getting to lodestar standards doesn't happen by itself and we have to make an active programme and implement it and work hard at it to get ourselves to that level.

This programme—to grow yourself to lodestar levels—can be narrowed down to four steps:

1. Define the lodestar standard for that value.
2. Identify a few areas for targeted practice.
3. Broaden the areas for practice to a wider set of areas.
4. Embed them fully in your daily behaviour.

The first step is **defining the lodestar standard for the value** you have chosen. For e.g., say you chose the value of commitment. You could define for yourself that the lodestar standard of commitment is keeping your word 100 per cent of the time you give it, and that you would rather not make a commitment if you are not sure you can keep it. I will give you another example from my own journey. I had personally chosen 'honesty' as one of my lodestar values and the box below would give you an idea of how I defined my lodestar standard for that value.

The challenge with honesty is that everyone considers themselves honest and that is because there isn't a defined standard for honesty. In the absence of a standard, we set our standards of honesty based on what others do; if a large majority of society is doing something then that becomes acceptable and honest, irrespective of whether in reality it is 'right' or 'wrong'. I personally chose to say that the lodestar standard for honesty would be to decide whether something is 'right' or 'wrong' based on morality and not on what others thought/did. I had a similar concept in *Catalyst* which I have depicted in the diagram below.

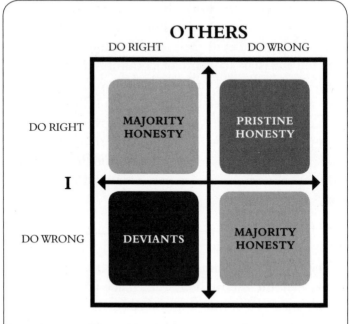

As you can see from this diagram, the majority of the population falls into what I call the 'majority honesty' quadrant—they do right when everyone else is doing right, but they don't mind doing wrong if everyone else is doing the same wrong thing. When they take such actions that society generally considers acceptable, they don't think of themselves as dishonest. For example, take the piracy of books, software and music. Most people don't mind downloading a pirated version of a book, music, movies, software, etc. Piracy effectively cheats the people involved in the sale of that item of the income they would have received if the item had been purchased legitimately. Now, since a large majority of people do it, we do not think of it as wrong to cheat in this way and when we use a pirated product of any kind, we do not think that makes us dishonest. But those same people would not consider it to be okay to steal a few hundred rupees from someone's wallet because society considers that to be unacceptable and dishonest. If you think about it, piracy also has the same result—we are cheating someone of a few hundred rupees. Yet, we don't see these two actions in the same light. This happens because we set our standards of honesty not based on what is 'right' or 'wrong,' but based on what others do. Hence, since the majority of people don't mind piracy, we feel that it is okay.

To achieve lodestar standards in honesty, I had to define my honesty as the one in the pristine honesty quadrant—I shall do 'right' even when others do 'wrong'. I had to stand out from the majority honesty quadrant of people.

Creating your own definition for the lodestar standards of the value you chose is a personal process, and you need to decide how you can stand out from everyone else through this value.

Once you define the lodestar standards for your value, then the **second step is identifying a few areas for targeted practice**. No one can achieve lodestar standards in their chosen values overnight. It takes practice. Choose an area where you will first focus on practising this value. It could be at home, at work, with your friends, or wherever else you like. Going back to our commitment example from earlier, you could start by saying that you will keep every commitment you make to your family, be it for a movie or dinner or parent teacher meeting or coming back home early on a certain day. As you start to practise in a few targeted areas, you will become more self-aware of your current standing in that value and start recognizing the challenges of maintaining such high standards and what you must do to overcome them.

Once you feel confident in your ability to practise those values at their lodestar levels within your targeted area, move towards **step three, which is broadening the areas you seek to practise the value**. So, for e.g., for commitment, you can broaden from family to colleagues at work and say that 'any commitment that I make to my colleagues at work, I will keep'.

In a way, what this is doing is building your muscle for practising this value at a higher level. We can't lift a 50-kg weight in a gym exercise on the first day. We have to start with 5 kg and slowly build our muscles to lift 10 kg, then 20, then 40, then 50 kg. In the same way, slowly widen your range of practice as you feel more comfortable with each area.

Do this until you reach the **final step which is the embedding stage** where you start to practise that value at a lodestar standard in all areas. Use the muscle you have built to make this your daily life, to the extent that it does not take conscious effort from you on a day-to-day basis to practise this value.

One final thing about values-based leadership—it is like compound interest; it takes time to grow and become powerful. The early stages of practising values-based leadership may not create any great impact, but slowly and surely, it grows and once it reaches critical mass, it becomes the most powerful leadership tool you can have. That critical mass point is when the 'who' says it starts to matter more than 'what' is being said. And importantly, you also have built the values to never misuse that leadership impact and trust that people are giving you. I would urge you to walk down this path, because it is so less-trodden that your leadership will truly emerge as a giant amongst pygmies if you can summon the will, the heart and the soul to go down a values-based leadership path.

Behaviour towards people

As mentioned earlier, your people will continuously observe three things about you as you lead—your values, your behaviour towards people and your role modelling on challenging issues. Let us now turn our attention to the 'behaviour towards people' aspect.

One of the basic drivers about us as humans is that we choose to follow certain people as leaders based on observing how they treat their fellow humans. We do have a greater willingness to follow those leaders who we think treat other people decently. Occasionally, a leader can create followership by fear and intimidation such as treating a few people badly and using them to set an example, thereby forcing others to follow. However, that leader and their impact cannot last forever, nor is it powerful enough to drive transformational journeys. For us to win the respect of our teams, we have to treat people decently.

As we spend time at work, our focus tends to get diverted towards the business issue at hand. We are not very conscious of our body language, our behaviour towards others, and how we are treating people. These happen naturally, dictated by our subconscious and our habits, based on the 'being' we are. While we are not conscious about it, it does not mean that others are not consciously observing these things about us. As said earlier, a leader is always on stage, and people are observing your behaviour—are you being aggressive with someone, are you disinterested and looking at your mobile when someone is talking or presenting to you, are you interrupting rudely or listening well to what others have to say, are you open to ideas or do you want to impose only what's on your mind, etc. People observe every part of us as a leader, even when we are not aware and conscious about these things ourselves.

There are many behaviours of ours, known and unknown, and it is possibly not practical to look at every one of them. So, as always, I have tried to prioritize three things in the way you behave with people for you to focus on:

1. Respect
2. Fairness
3. Connection

While a lot of our behaviour towards others is driven by our subconscious, it is important to stay aware of these three areas and try and improve our behaviour to the best extent possible. However, the implementation and practice of such behaviours is not often defined well—they are concepts we all have a vague generic understanding of. So what I am going to try is to give you just one principle in each which I have practised that can potentially help you.

Respect

Respect, in the simplest terms, is about treating people respectfully irrespective of their position and importance. The one principle I want to give you is this: *When we become a leader, that position gives us a set of stated and **unstated** privileges. The stated privileges are rights in decision-making, perks, etc. It is the unstated privileges, which when misused, can result in disrespectful behaviour from our side.*

Let me give you some examples of unstated privileges that can be misused.

1. A leader can get angry and impatient and shout at a person they are leading—it is an unstated privilege. Can that person, when they get angry and impatient, have the same right to shout at the leader?

2. A leader can give an appointment to a junior person and keep that person waiting for an hour because they are busy with something else. This is an unstated privilege. Can a junior person keep a senior person waiting in return?

The list can go on and you can draw your own list of unstated privileges that can be misused. The challenge for a lot of leaders is not being aware of the subtler and subconscious forms of disrespect they practise because of these unstated privileges. I would urge you to become aware of which unstated privileges you may be exercising in the wrong way and put a stop to them. It is absolutely legitimate to use stated privileges. In fact, it is part of the leader's job, so do not get confused about that. It's the unstated privileges which build up due to the history and cultures of organizations, which the leader can wrongly assume as actual, legitimate privileges that they can exercise, that we should become aware of and correct.

Fairness

Fairness encompasses a variety of things. I think the most important area to be fair in is people decisions—how we enforce accountability and how we make decisions like promotions, salaries, transfers, etc. The one principle here that I will give you is this: *The people decisions you make must stand up to scrutiny by others. If an objective third person who had the exact same information and understanding you have were to evaluate that decision, would they find it fair, or would they find some of your personal biases in it?*

Let me give you some examples to bring this alive.

1. When performance is poor because of uncontrollable reasons and yet, you choose to let out your frustration by holding someone personally accountable.

2. When your apportioning of credits for good performance and the debits for poor performance across people is not based on objectivity but on your own biases.
3. When people with whom you have stronger personal relationships have a higher chance of being promoted and having better careers.
4. If the rules and principles based on which you make people decisions keep changing based on your convenience.

Again, you can add to the list. The key is that people decisions made by leaders are scrutinized whether we like it or not; every promotion decision you make, every transfer will be scrutinized and discussed by people. Usually, they can easily make out when you are being unfair, even if you think you are being clever about it. Sometimes, a decision you may make might be a fair decision, but it might be seen to be unfair because of non-transparent communication. So, transparency, consistency and setting the rules in advance, and communicating that well to people can help avoid some of these issues and help you be seen as a fair leader.

Connection

This is about the connection we make with the wider set of people we lead and is amongst the most challenging parts of being a leader. Here, I will do a little bit of cheating with my own rules and give you two principles.

Principle 1: The more people who feel they are personally known by the leader, the more effective the leadership is. The key here is being known personally, not because of the position they have in the company, but as a person.

Principle 2: The more people feel that you 'care', the more effective the connection.

I will give you some examples of how I practised this and some of the challenges as well.

1. Giving someone that sense of connection that they are personally known by the leader starts with trying to remember their names. When someone very senior in the company meets me and I don't have to introduce myself because they already know me, it builds a great connection. The same thing applies to our teams. Now this is an area I have struggled with, and honestly, in my early years, I did not care enough to do something about it as a leader. But with time, as I realized its importance, I started to make deliberate efforts to improve this. When I visited a factory or sales office, I would ask my assistant to give me a printout of the organizational chart with pictures of people and names. I would use some time in the flight to familiarize myself with that. Even now, when I do workshops with external companies, I often go through LinkedIn profiles of some people from there so that, during the session, I can build some connection.

2. Caring is simply about feeling and showing that '*I care about you, and I care about what you do for the company*'.

Some of things I have learnt from my mentors is to allow some time at the start of a meeting for free-flowing chat instead of jumping straight to business issues and the agenda. A few simple questions like, 'How are you?', 'What are some of the exciting things you are doing at work?' and then listening to those answers well can go a long way in letting people know that 'I care about what you do'.

Role modelling on difficult, challenging and complex issues

Apart from your values and behaviour towards people, the third thing people observe in you as a leader is your personal stance and actions on difficult things. How is our role modelling in those areas? Are we asking people to do what we are not doing ourselves or are we willing to be a role model and lead from the front on difficult issues?

Role modelling as a concept is well known. The key question as a leader is what are the areas that you are focusing on role modelling. The one principle for me is that *role modelling is most important when you do it for difficult and complex issues; when you do it in leading change. You have to model not what people are already doing but what you want them to do differently in the future.*

I want to share a story on how powerful the impact of role modelling can be. This was when I was in Asian Paints. P.M. Murty (PMM), who retired as the MD of Asian Paints, was one of the senior-most leaders then. Asian Paints, in those days, was not very strong in automobile paints and most of the cars made in the country were not painted with Asian Paints. The company car policy for employees was, however, liberal, and we could buy any car as per our eligibility, irrespective of what brand of paint it used. Once, when the car policy was upgraded with higher eligibilities, PMM was very clear that he would only buy a car which used Asian Paints. This meant that he had to make trade-offs on his eligibility on the type of car, the colour choices he had and even had to wait longer for the delivery of the car. But this was his role modelling on commitment to the company and the brand. He never said anything to others about it, but he was a visible role model—there for all to see. As I said, the story is about the impact role modelling has on people, and this is about the impact PMM's role modelling had on me. When I joined Onida, I had two TVs at home of another brand. But within months of joining, I changed both to Onida despite the cost I had to bear. And when I joined Cadbury, I remember telling my daughter Prerana, who was very young then, that if she went to a kid's birthday party and the chocolates they gave there were not Cadbury, she could not eat them. Role modelling by the leader impacts people fundamentally, and can even change their values. So, believe in the power of your role modelling.

Here are some examples of how I practised role modelling to lead change in a few areas:

1. Some of the organizations I worked in were quite hierarchical with excessive respect and fear of the boss and leaders above. I have always been clear in my mind that hierarchical cultures impede organizational

effectiveness. They reduce open communication and, most importantly, people do not often transparently communicate the problems they face. To break the symbolism of hierarchy, I decided and communicated that no one could call me 'sir'. They had to call me by name, whatever level in the company they were. I did this in two different companies. It would take a lot of cajoling and some friendly fines at times, but in both companies, the culture changed slowly to being more friendly with more open flows of communication and less hierarchy. It was also a message to my team—I did not tell them that they had to be less hierarchical, but my role modelling was a clear message to them.

2. When I was in HR at Cadbury, gender diversity was big on the agenda. While diversity has come a long way now beyond just gender to focus on multiple groups and inclusion as an agenda, in those days, we were focused on gender diversity. One day, one of my best female team members came to me and said she had to quit because her husband had got a job in another city, and she had to relocate there. I said, 'While we don't have HR roles in that city, why can't you just do your current job from home in the new city?' (WFH is fashionable now, but it was certainly not so twelve–thirteen years ago). It took a lot of discussions, but we were finally able to make it work and she worked from home from the other city. Now, this was something that had never been done before in the company, and it sent a message that we were serious about gender diversity and as a leader, I was willing to walk the extra mile for that.

Role modelling on difficult issues and change agendas is important. The simple thing that people look for is, are you 'being' what you are asking them to 'be' like. If you are 'being' someone else, and your actions are different from the words you speak, different from what you are asking people to do, then you would be ineffective as a leader. It is important to align how we are—our 'being'—with how we are asking our people to 'be'. And this is particularly important in difficult and challenging issues. When we are driving complex change, we have to change before we get others to change.

Authentic leadership

We discussed authentic leadership right in the beginning of this book, but I need to bring it back once again in this context.

In a way, authentic leadership is essentially the practice of an elevated form of 'leading by being'. When the nature of your 'being' is so attractive and magnetic to others that they are inspired by the person you are and follow you as a leader, you naturally become an authentic leader. *You are who you are, and others accept your leadership because of who you are.* After reading this, authentic leadership could seem very easy—all I have to do is be myself and I become an authentic leader. The catch lies in the fact that your 'being yourself' has to be inspiring, attractive and magnetic to others. If our being ourselves is not inspiring, attractive and magnetic to others, then we might be authentic to who we are, but we won't be leaders. To that extent, authentic leadership is not easy, because you have to grow your 'being' to that level which is aspirational and inspirational for others.

Does it mean that you have to be perfect to be authentic? No, authentic leaders have their weaknesses as well, but what makes them aspirational is that they don't try and hide their weaknesses, their shortcomings. That willingness to be vulnerable, that willingness not to appear to be the perfect leader, is actually an important part of the package of being an authentic leader. A perfect person can appear fake, can appear put on and non-genuine and the truth is that, in reality, no one is perfect. Authentic leaders are authentic even about their shortcomings and that makes them human, and hence more effective in leading, since these are people with great strengths that help them overcome even these weaknesses.

While one does not have to be perfect, there is a lot of common agreement across literature on some of the **minimum standards** of being an authentic leader. The common ones quoted across literature are:

1. Authentic leaders tend to be high integrity leaders. It is difficult to be low integrity and 'be yourself' and get accepted as an authentic leader.
2. Authentic leaders practise honesty in relationships and feedback. They communicate the truth when giving feedback; they don't sugarcoat bad messages and don't shy away from giving genuine, positive feedback as well when it is due. Most importantly, they are willing to take honest feedback themselves.

3. Authentic leaders are outcome and long-term focused. As it is said, authentic leaders are very aware of who they are and where they come from, but equally, they are very focused on where they need to go.

4. And of course, the most important—authentic leaders are being true to who they are while doing the above. A very significant requirement for this is high self-awareness.

So, what should you do to be an authentic leader? The starting point is self-awareness of where we are now as a 'human being'. All of us would like to believe that we are good human beings, but as I said, the catch is that 'our being' should be aspirational and inspirational to others. If there is nothing about our personalities, our character, our human qualities which is inspiring to others, then frankly, there are a few million other people like that. As said previously, authentic leadership is quite simply the most elevated form of practising *leadership by being*. Hence, it does not require any new tools. All it requires is that you practise the various leadership tools I have spoken about at an elevated level, particularly in regard to the *leading by being* aspect.

In my workshops, I often get asked many questions on barriers to authentic leadership. The most common question is, 'By nature, I am an introverted person. Is it still possible to be an authentic leader?' Whether you are introverted or extroverted is a part of who you are, and authenticity demands that you be who you are and not act like someone else. The real issue is whether it becomes a barrier to the minimum standards described earlier. For e.g., one of the minimum standards is communicating feedback truthfully and clearly to the people you work with. If your introversion prevents you from engaging people for giving them feedback or taking feedback, then it is a barrier to you becoming an authentic leader. But, if your introversion does not prevent you from engaging and communicating honestly with people when required, then introversion is not a barrier to leadership. It is a part of your authentic self. So, if you are somewhat introverted, you need not worry. You can still be an authentic leader, be aware of the minimum standards and don't let your introversion become a barrier to that.

Sometimes, the question is, 'I am not very strategic, but I am very good at getting the job done. Can I become a great leader?' Again, the question is whether it is a barrier for the minimum standards. One of the minimum standards is the ability to be long-term focused which means you need to have a sense of vision and direction for the long term. As long as you can create a vision and direction for the future, you can be a great leader.

So essentially, the message is that the minimum standards are required to be fulfilled. As long as you are able to meet the minimum standards while being who you are, you have no need to try and change yourself. However, if you are not able to meet the minimum standards, then there is an imperative that you identify that area and work to improve on it over time, such that it becomes a part of the new 'authentic you'.

Chapter summary:

1. A leader is always on stage and people are observing you all the time. A lot of your leadership impact is based on how people perceive you as a 'human being'. They are observing your values, your behaviour towards other people and your role modelling on challenging and complex issues. When your 'being' becomes powerful, people start following 'you' the person, increasing your leadership impact.

2. As per the VML equation, **V**alue **M**ultiplies **L**eadership.

   Leadership impact = (Position + Content) x Values.

   Leading is the act of getting people to follow you on a journey. People follow based on 'what' is being said/asked and 'who' is saying it. Values multiply the power of the 'who' saying it and that is why they are such an important driver for leadership impact.

3. The best way to leverage values to create leadership impact is to develop a couple of lodestar values which you practise at a level that is head and shoulders above anyone else. The steps to choosing the lodestar values are:

   a. Identify five–seven of your core values.
   b. From those, choose two to be your lodestar values based on the context you are in and the likely impact of that value in that context.

4. Just because we have chosen a lodestar value does not mean we are practising it already at lodestar levels. To do that, you have to build a programme.

   a. Define the lodestar standard for that value.
   b. Identify a few areas for targeted practice.
   c. Broaden the areas for practice to a wider set of areas.
   d. Embed them fully in your daily behaviour.

5. One of the important things people observe about us as leaders is how we treat other people and our behaviour towards them. Three things matter:

   a. Respect
   b. Fairness
   c. Connection

6. Role modelling is most powerful when you do it in difficult and complex issues; when you do it in leading change. You have to role model not what people are already doing but what you want them to do differently in the future.

7. Authentic leaders lead in a way which is a true reflection of themselves and an elevated practice of 'leading by being'. Authenticity is about being true to the nature of your 'being', but leadership comes only when that 'being' is perceived as attractive and inspirational for others to follow. The minimum standards to be an authentic leader are:

  a. Being high on integrity.
  b. Being honest in relationships and in communicating with people.
  c. Being outcome and long-term focused.
  d. Being true to yourself and being highly self-aware of who you really are.

8. Leadership by being is a slow process and it is about putting in continuous deposits. But once it reaches critical mass, then it is much more powerful than any other leadership tool you have because 'who' says it acquires great weight. So make a determined effort to be the best 'being' you can be.

11

Crisis Leadership, Entrepreneurial Leadership and Leadership Is for Everyone

It was October 2003. The year had so far gone well for Cadbury and for Bharat Puri, the then MD of the company. Then, a news story broke that there were worms found in Cadbury chocolates and all hell broke loose. News channels and newspapers started giving headline coverage to the story. In a very short time, it became a full-blown crisis, the kind of crisis that you would not wish on anyone. Sales fell by over 70 per cent in many markets; it felt like the business was collapsing and everything was doom and gloom. And yet, within one year, the business turned around, and by 2005, it was back to growth. In a few years, it felt like the crisis had receded to the background and no one even remembered it. How did that happen? It was thanks to the extraordinary leadership of Bharat in that crisis; a crisis which looked like it would take the company down with it. Not only was the crisis overcome in a short period, the company flourished after that. We can learn a lot of leadership lessons from Bharat and how he handled this crisis.

The early stages of any crisis are truly the worst—it feels like the end of the world is near and things can't get worse. It was no different for Bharat and Cadbury at that time. Every single day, the story was on prime time television and in the newspapers. Politicians got into the act; there were protests outside Cadbury House (the then headquarters of the company in Mumbai) and in fact, some of the protestors wanted to blacken Bharat's face with paint. Magazines printed Bharat's cartoons with some very unkind captions. Every day, many calls would be received from people threatening that they had a video of worms in Cadbury chocolates, and if the company did not pay them money, they would give it to the media. Production was grinding to a halt. Retailers lost confidence and stopped selling the company's products. Consumer acceptance of the company's brands collapsed. It felt like a perfect storm. Typical of the early stage of any crisis, problems came flying from all sides and there was no respite in sight. As a leader, you could get engulfed in the storm. But if you are the kind of leader that is going to stand tall as a lighthouse and show your teams the direction they must take, even as the storm blows, you will naturally be a far superior leader. And that is what Bharat did. He stood tall right from the initial stages.

I have had many conversations with Bharat on this crisis, and through all those conversations, this is what

I gleaned. The first and foremost thing that Bharat did was to decide that while there were a lot of issues flying at him every day, the important thing was to not get distracted in dealing with each and every little situation. Instead, it was important to get to the root cause of the issue—why do worms get into chocolate? He wanted to solve that problem, and devise a solution to prevent worms from going in, so that the consumers could have a better experience. That ability of Bharat, to keep his focus on solving the root cause, was remarkable. He could have easily spent a lot of his time on PR management—managing incidents, giving press interviews, etc. Instead, he chose to focus his energies on solving the root cause which was about how to prevent the worms from going inside the packaging of the chocolate.

Once he built that clarity, the most important task was to get the people and the organization galvanized to solve the problem. There was a lot of demotivation and also some fear on whether the company would ever be able to come out of this crisis. People needed to lose the fear and build confidence that the company would be able to solve this problem. Bharat formulated four principles in this situation:

1. *We will accept the existence of the problem and not dispute whether the problem exists.* This was a master stroke of leadership. Many companies, when faced with crises and product problems, often start with saying, 'Our products are perfect. There is no problem.' Bharat turned this on its head and said, 'We will accept that there is a problem.' This acceptance made sure that

no time was wasted in deciding whether there *was* a problem. Instead, the focus shifted to how to solve the problem.

2. *No head will roll for this crisis. I want everyone together, solving the problem, not criticizing each other on who was responsible for it.* In a great crisis like this, there is also a lot of discussion within organizations on who is accountable for the problem, which heads are going to roll, etc. Bharat understood that if people are insecure, if people start playing politics to protect themselves, then the organization will distract itself from solving the core problem. He made it clear that criticizing each other and playing politics was pointless. It was truly remarkable—considering the scale of the crisis—that not a single person was asked to leave the company. By doing that, Bharat made sure that the organization was united in solving the problem, not fighting each other.

3. *We will do whatever it takes to solve the core issue and we will do it with speed.* Solving the issue was the only priority. All the hesitation and boundary conditions had to be ignored during this period. Things like 'we have not done it in the past', 'what is the cost', 'we don't know how to do it', etc. would not be allowed to come in the way.

4. *Complete transparency within the company through regular communication.* We often see how a set of senior people meet in conference rooms during a crisis every day, and the rest of the company is often left unaware. Bharat wanted complete and transparent communication, and himself stood up and communicated repeatedly to

the organization on the issue, and what the company was doing.

Bharat's leadership team, comprising some very high-quality people, and the rest of the organization responded to his leadership. The company quickly created new packaging which would prevent the worms from going into the chocolate. Packing machines, which otherwise would take eighteen months to import and install, were imported and installed in just six months. Once the new product with the new packaging was ready, the next issue of solving low consumer confidence and retailer confidence had to be tackled. Consumer confidence was solved for by the masterstroke of getting celebrated actor Amitabh Bachchan as the brand ambassador. Retailer confidence was restored through what was known as Project Vishwaas (Trust). Company personnel went to each retailer, took old stocks back, gave them new stocks, and communicated about the packaging changes made. In many cases, where retailers still lacked confidence, the company representative would open a bar of chocolate and eat it right in front of them to build confidence that there was nothing wrong and it was perfectly edible. Thanks to all these actions, the company started recovering from the crisis within a year; sales slowly started climbing back, consumer and retailer confidence started reviving, and slowly but steadily, the company was chugging at full speed again.

Let me summarize some of the leadership lessons that you and I can learn from what Bharat did as a leader in this crisis.

1. As a leader, you have to **focus on the core problem that created the crisis and solve that**. There would be hundreds of other ancillary problems and noise during a crisis, but if you get distracted by them, then you will not solve the core problem and you will not overcome the crisis. There will be a lot of pressure and pull from ancillary problems drawing your attention, but as a leader, you must stay resolutely focused on the core problem.

2. The early stages of a crisis are the darkest, and as a leader, you might not even be clear about what is to be done. This is the time to stand tall, to build hope, to build belief that we can overcome the situation. When everyone is down, the leader must stand tall.

3. Crises require that leaders lead from the front. Bharat is normally a team player and would typically stand behind his team as they did the work. But in a crisis scenario, he recognized that he had to lead from the front. A crisis requires that, as leaders, we take accountability, take the problem head-on and not deflect it, and show visible leadership from the front in solving the crisis. Lead from the front and lead with taking full accountability in a crisis.

4. Sometimes, in a crisis, there is a lot of focus on finding the business solution, but not enough focus on the organizational and people side of a crisis. Crises impact organizational motivation and effectiveness tremendously, and as a leader, you are not going to solve the problem simply by finding the business solution. As a crisis leader, you must focus on energizing the organization as well, getting people

back on their feet to solve the problem, working with each other as a team, etc.

The last thing I learnt from Bharat was how valuable a crisis can be in your leadership development journey. When you are in the middle of a crisis it feels like, 'Oh my god, why am I in this?' But when you successfully come out of a crisis, you realize that you have grown significantly both as a leader and as a person. Bharat often used to tell us about the visit of the global chairman of Cadbury during that time. And the chairman told him, 'Bharat, you are a very lucky man that you are going through this crisis.' Bharat would often joke and say, 'What has this man been smoking? I am going through hell here and he says I am lucky?!' It was only later that he realized how powerful that crisis was in shaping him into becoming the successful and extraordinary leader that he now is. I don't want to wish a crisis on you, but if one does happen, face it with full energy and full capability, don't shy away from it—it can radically grow you and transform you as a leader.

The entrepreneurial context

Entrepreneurship is alive and kicking in the world—we are in the age of start-ups. Many younger people would rather be founders than just work at a corporate for a long time. They bring tremendous energy, great passion, a can-do attitude and some great ideas. But at the same time, many of them are young, with not enough grey hair on their heads and haven't necessarily gone through a leadership learning journey. As I work with start-ups, I find that there are three imperatives that the founder(s) must understand in their practice of leadership.

1. In the beginning, the founder(s) is involved in everything. There is nothing that happens in the start-up that the founder is not aware of and not involved in—they know every nut and bolt. In effect, they are 100 per cent in managing mode and zero per cent in leading mode to start with. They are directly involved in everything. However, a start-up can change and grow at a rapid pace and very soon, it might reach a stage where the founder cannot be directly involved in everything. Many founders fail to recognize this transition, stay in a primarily managing mode, and do not add a leading dimension to what they do. Recognizing when the transition happens and consciously changing yourself from just managing to leading *and* managing is the first imperative for an entrepreneur/founder.

2. Start-ups often work with limited resources. Where fifty people are required, they make do with thirty-five. This means that each of those thirty-five has to work with a very high level of effectiveness. As a founder, your means to getting them to work at a higher level of effectiveness is VISA. If each of those thirty-five understands the vision, is inspired to give it their best, is clear about the strategy and is aligned on the priorities, then they are going to be a lot more effective. However, I find that founders are so busy operationally that they don't take the time

to lead, they don't take the time to do what it takes to give the VISA to their teams. They don't take the time to build and communicate a shared vision, inspire people, build and communicate strategic clarity which remains largely within their heads, or drive alignment on priorities. The operational requirements of the job are so high that these things are given the short end of the stick, but they are exactly what are required. When you work with constrained human resources, then each person has to be more effective and VISA is the answer to that, and taking the time and the energy out to do that is the second imperative.

3. The founder's impact on the culture and ethos of an organization—its soft side—is extraordinary. In most start-ups, the founder's personality is equal to the culture of the organization. In effect, how the founders are 'being' today is how the start-up will 'be' tomorrow. This implies that the highest impact of leading by being is in an entrepreneurial context. As a founder, you must be very aware that your 'being' is shaping your company's being for the future, and hence, it is imperative that you are at your best 'being' today. This is also an opportunity; if as a founder, I have a vision of the kind of culture, ethos and values my company should have in the future, then the first thing I have to do is to build those things into the nature of the person I am. Without me authentically reflecting all those values, my company will never become what I want it to become.

Entrepreneurship, becoming a founder, and initiating and growing a start-up is an extraordinary journey and experience in a person's life. Certainly, many start-ups succeed and those are the poster children we keep hearing about. But for every one that succeeds, there are many that don't. And as I observe—now this might sound harsh—often, it is not the start-up but the founder who fails. Sometimes, it could be that the business idea was not scalable, but many a time, it is quite simply the founder not recognizing the three imperatives listed above. Not recognizing that as they grow, they can't just be managing but have to add leading to managing, not recognizing that being operationally busy all the time does not make your people more effective, and to make them more effective you have to take the time out and give them the VISA and lastly, not recognizing that some of the negative aspects of their personality and their 'being' are adversely impacting the start-up and they have to change themselves for the start-up to flourish.

Everyone must lead and everyone must be led

One of the challenges of writing on the topic of leadership is that it can feel like it is largely aimed at those who have become senior people in their careers, and that it is not relevant to the juniors. Earlier in the book, I tried to disabuse this notion and I want to do this again; everyone must lead, including the juniors. There are several junior jobs where there is actually a large contingent of people you are leading—imagine a junior engineer on a construction site, a junior sales manager heading a sales team, a warehouse manager heading a large team, an e-commerce manager leading a large front-end delivery team, a store manager of a modern trade store, etc. No matter how junior your role is, if you have a large team, then you have to be able to lead them.

What about those who are junior but don't have a team, can they also lead? Leading is about impacting those people and actions where you are not closely involved. When you think of it that way, then even as a junior you should learn to impact people and actions where you are not closely involved, including impacting people who are your peers and senior to you, impacting the strategy of the company, etc. When you do that, it is a leadership action. I've generally noticed that while senior people work on formulating strategies, they make a point of visualizing a junior employee who would implement that strategy, so as to be able to understand the response of the implementation teams. Often, they are picturing a specific junior or a few juniors that they know; it won't be all the juniors. In a way, that specific junior is having an impact on the senior, even without being directly involved in the strategy, which is how we have defined leading. Never forget what I keep saying: *the people who become leaders are those who started leading before they were called leaders.* Start leading now irrespective of your job title and where you stand in the hierarchy.

The second mistaken notion is that certain groups of people don't need to be led. These are people especially at the lowest end of the hierarchy, for e.g., they could be workers in a factory, construction workers, the large force of delivery agents in e-commerce, the employees of your distributors who actually make the sale, etc. A lot of the focus of leaders is in leading executives and managers within the company. There is somehow a sense that at the lowest level of the hierarchy, it is very transactional, and there is very little effort put in to lead those teams. *My belief is everyone needs to be led.* In fact, one could look at it the other way; executives and managers can still self-motivate and inspire themselves, but at the lowest levels of the hierarchy, they do need help to motivate themselves. We somehow tend to think that things like vision and inspiration are not important to this group. But think of it this way, if a construction worker or a factory worker can actually have a vision and get inspired, then how much would be the impact? Currently, they work in a very transactional way. But if they were actually engaged and inspired, then the extent to which they can lift up the quantity and quality of their work could be very high. There is a very high return for leadership with this group of people, since it often directly impacts major factors like productivity or sales of the organization. However, we have to be willing to acknowledge them as an important group of people, and put in some effort to lead them, and engage their hearts and minds. It's very easy for us to neglect this group, particularly when they are off-roll employees of the company, but if we want to see our leadership impact the organization from the very top to the very bottom, we will have to keep in mind that even as junior managers, our role to play is critical.

Chapter summary:

1. A crisis may be among the toughest challenges you would face in your life but it is also an opportunity to grow as a leader and as a person. To successfully lead in a crisis:

    a. Keep your focus on the core problem that caused the crisis and solve it. Don't let the noise and ancillary problems distract you.
    b. The early stages of a crisis are the darkest and that is the time you must stand tall and build hope and belief.
    c. Lead from the front, take the problem on your chin and don't deflect it to others.
    d. Only a business solution won't be enough. In parallel, you must revive the organization and the people.

2. To be successful at leading in an entrepreneurial context, the founder has to recognize three imperatives:

    a. Transition from 100 per cent managing to leading and managing as the start-up grows and gains scale.
    b. Take time out to give VISA to your people to make them more effective. Your being operationally busy does not grow the effectiveness of your people.
    c. Your 'being' is going to impact the future culture of the company. Be aware of it and consciously

      practise those values and ethos that you wish to see in your company.

3. Leadership is not only for seniors but also for juniors. If you manage a large contingent of people even as a junior, then it is vital that you lead. And for those juniors who don't have people in their teams, they can still lead. Leading is the act of impacting where you are not involved and you can impact your peers, your seniors, etc.

4. Everyone must be led. Sometimes, the lowest hierarchy tends to be ignored. However, the opportunity for leadership and the impact of the leadership is very high with that group of people. Whoever has an impact on your and the company's performance must be led however low in the hierarchy they are and sometimes, even if they are outside the company.

Summary: Section 3 and Introduction to Section 4

In the last four chapters, we have covered a series of transformations you need to make to become good at leading. The first is to understand that just because you are called a leader, does not mean you are leading. One of the great fallacies is that 'actions of leaders = leadership'. Instead, you must focus on leading as defined, which is the art of impacting people and their actions where you have limited involvement. The second important transformation is to recognize that as we become senior, and as a lesser percentage of our performance is in our control, we have to move from just managing, to managing and leading, and increase the time we allocate for leading. The two ways to lead are 'leading by doing' and 'leading by being'.

Leading by doing enables you to achieve two outcomes; firstly, it helps your people build a narrative and meaning for what they do at work, and secondly, it helps you guide their actions when you are not involved. You do this by giving them a VISA—Vision, Inspiration, Strategic clarity and Alignment. V and I typically help your people build the narrative and meaning for what they do at work while S and A help guide their actions when you are not involved.

Leading by being is a very powerful aspect of leadership. It is about the nature of person you are, the 'being' you are and how you can inspire and attract people to follow you and accept your leadership. Leading by being can be built by developing your values-based leadership impact through building a couple of lodestar values where you are head and shoulders above everyone else. The right behaviour towards other people by being respectful, fair in people decisions and building a connection, coupled with role modelling from the front on difficult issues and areas where you want to drive change can grow your leadership impact further. Authentic leadership, in a way, is the ultimate form of leadership by being, where you are just being true to yourself, but your being yourself is so attractive and inspiring for others that they follow you as a leader.

This brings us to an important point—how do we connect leading with business? Let us ask ourselves what the outcomes are that we want to impact for the business through our leadership. At a macro level, I have listed four outcomes which our leadership must impact:

1. Performance—short-term and sustainable longer-term performance.
2. Strategy—guiding people on what we do and how we do it to drive the above performance.
3. Employees—getting greater commitment and engagement from them, leaving them more inspired and motivated and having a sense of meaning at work.
4. Culture—defining who we are as a group of people and company and how we work by ourselves and with each other. Impacting the intangibles which are important for the business but can't be measured easily.

If I am leading well, then my leadership actions should impact these four outcomes positively. Let us try and make a connection between what we have discussed in the previous chapters and connect that to the following table:

Business outcomes to impact through leadership	Achieving these outcomes 'by'	Leading by doing—VISA	Leading by being		
Performance—short and long term	Guiding the actions of people when you are not directly involved or not there	Providing S and A, i.e., Strategic clarity and Alignment		Role modelling on difficult and complex change issues can impact all the business outcomes based on what is being role modelled	Values-based leadership impact happens by amplifying the voice of the leader on all leading acts they do by growing the power of the 'who'
Strategy—guiding people on the 'what' and the 'how'					
Employee engagement and commitment	Helping people build a narrative and meaning for what they do at work	Providing V and I; Vision and Inspiration	Behaviour towards people		
Impacting culture					

Hopefully this table helps you connect different leading actions with how they impact the outcomes for the business.

Leading by doing impacts employee engagement and commitment, as well as culture, through the Vision and Inspiration the leader provides, and impacts business performance and guides the actions of people on strategy through providing Strategic clarity and driving Alignment. To that extent, VISA is crucial; the content of the VML equation lies here.

Leading by being operates differently with various aspects having diverse types of impact. Good behaviour with people encompassing respect, fairness and connection helps build employee engagement and commitment and it impacts culture as well. Role modelling has the potential to impact all the business outcomes based on what role the leader is modelling. Values-based leadership impact is the most important and unique one. It primarily works as an amplifier. Imagine a megaphone in the hands of a leader—it amplifies the power of everything the leader does because it has grown the power of 'who' over 'what'. To that extent, I always believe it is the most powerful leadership tool because of the extraordinary amplification it can provide to everything you do. Having said that, for a leader with poor values, it can also act as a de-amplifier, reducing the leadership impact of everything else they do.

Self-awareness: The master key

We've seen how leadership can impact your business outcomes. So, does that mean that to impact outcomes positively and to have great leadership impact, all you need to do is perform actions of leading by doing and leading by being? Largely yes, but with one caveat. There is one master key without which leading by doing and leading by being cannot be unlocked to get the full impact. That master key is called 'self-awareness'. Being exceptionally self-aware is vital to being able to practise leadership for higher impact.

There are three levels of self-awareness:

1. What others think of you.
2. What you think of yourself.
3. Who you really are and who are you at the core.

In most leadership programmes, there is almost always a lot of emphasis on growing self-awareness. This is often done through 360-degree surveys and helps create a great awareness of what other people think of you as well as captures what you think of yourself. You also get a gap analysis on which areas are the ones where what you think of yourself is very different from what other people think of you. This is valuable, as getting a grounded understanding of what others think of you is important to calibrating and growing the impact of your leading actions over time. So, every time you get an opportunity for a 360-degree survey, please utilize it with all focus and seriousness. Over and above 360s, I have personally practised asking for direct feedback face-to-face in one-on-one meetings with people. I find this to sometimes be more powerful than 360s because a discussion is possible on the feedback which allows you to understand it better.

A 360 does not allow you to probe to understand the feedback better, but face-to-face feedback allows you to do that. However, this does require that you have the humility to ask for feedback; you are able to ask for it in a way which is non-threatening to the giver of the feedback, and you accept the feedback when it is given. Try practising it, since over and above just getting feedback, this helps improve the honest connection that you build with your people. So, a combination of a good 360 and some face-to-face feedback can help you answer the first two questions: 'what others think of you' and 'what you think of yourself'. The problem is that in most cases, self-awareness stops at this level; it does not progress to the most important third question.

To get to the highest form of leading by being, to become a truly authentic leader, you have to go beyond 'what you think of yourself' to understanding 'who you really are at the core'. Often, who we really are could be very different from who we think we are. 'What we think of ourselves' need not be factual, some of it is wishful. A very strong, grounded sense of awareness around 'who am I at the core', 'what motivates and drives me', 'what boundaries would I not cross whatever be the pressure and the challenge', 'what legacy do I seek to leave' are the kind of questions that you must have clear answers for. These are not often possible to decode via a 360. This requires deep introspection and reflection from your side. Many a time, even that does not get you to understanding your core. Instead, you end up stopping at your self-image of the core, i.e., what you want your core to be, not what your core really is. To get past that self-image problem and to understand your real core, you must validate your assessment of your core with your behaviour. Does what you do, your behaviour and actions, seem consistent with who you think you are? For e.g., if at the core, you feel you are a very kind and helpful person, then look back at the past month and see how many people you helped. Was that meaningful enough to justify the feeling that you are a kind and helpful person at the core, or is that just a self-image?

Understanding who you are at the core is like peeling an onion. There are many layers and it can be challenging, but the ultimate self-awareness journey is about decoding who you are at the core and it is not about what others think of you or what you think of yourself. So, all the very best in peeling the onion of the human being called 'you'.

SECTION 4

12

The Embedding Process, Converting Knowledge to Behaviour

We come to the final section now where I will bring everything together in a way that will help you put it into practice. I truly believe that there is no point in any framework or theory till you put it into practice, till it starts translating into your impact at work. So here is my attempt to make it simple for you, to put all that I have said in this book into practice.

Recap of the 'People' focus

In my book *Get Better at Getting Better,* I had articulated what I called the four core capabilities required for a person to become successful, and I have reproduced them here below:

1. People skills/relationships/leadership/personal value systems
2. Analytical skills/comfort with numbers/logical reasoning

3. Conceptualization and intuitive skills/creativity/ insightfulness
4. Organized/disciplined/planned/effective behaviour

As you can see, one of these capabilities you require is people-related—how you lead and manage people, how you build relationships, and how you are as a human being. I have often tried to figure out which of the four is most important and which is the least, and to rank them in order. In doing that, I uncovered some insights for myself.

The importance *does* vary based on the situation and the context. Also, most industries have stereotypes, but the ones who break those stereotypes are often the most successful. For example, a developer or a coder in the IT industry needs to be good at analytical skills, logical reasoning, etc. But analytical skills are merely the base requirement without which you don't even have a starting point. However, if that is all you have, then there a few million like you in that industry. You have to have a second or third strength from that list which gives you the edge over others for achieving success. Very few people develop their second or third strength, which is why the number of people truly getting to the top remains low. Similarly, if you are in a creative field, say advertising or content creation, you need to be good at conceptualization, creativity, etc. But that again, is a base requirement and everyone in those fields probably have these skills already. Again, people who become really successful are those who can add a second or third edge. For e.g., in creative fields, people may generate a lot of ideas, but can lack the discipline, planning and organization skills to focus on a few ideas and execute them well. So, those who add the second edge of being organized/disciplined/effective, are possibly going to be more successful.

As I studied and analysed this more, one thing became clear to me. People management skills were a near universal requirement in all industries, and their impact on making a person successful seemed quite high. In many companies, I found that the people at the top are not necessarily the most technically competent or the most creative, but they were almost always good leaders and managers—they were good at people management. It was difficult to find someone who had become a CEO but sucked at people management, although I am sure exceptions exist, especially in owner-/family-managed enterprises and at times, even at professionally managed companies. But they were ultimately exceptions; the norm I saw was that people who got to the top were generally good at being leaders and managers. So, the basic requirement to be very successful, no matter what field you're in, is to become good at people management. It is not an option to be poor at that.

The second thing I noticed was that people management was an area that most people were able to become good at as long as they made a determined effort to learn and improve. Sometimes, if you are very strong analytically, it can be challenging to learn to become very creative, since these mindsets can be conflicting. However, people management is an area which is complementary to all other capabilities. It is possible to become good at people management, and it does not clash with your other capabilities. In a way, people management is a capability which amplifies all your other capabilities. You might see that the person with the smartest technical capability does not get a leadership position because of their poor people management skills. Instead, someone who has decent technical capability which is sufficient to do the job, despite not necessarily being the best, gets to a leadership position because their strong people management skills amplify that technical capability. Many people with moderate business and technical capabilities are often very successful in their careers because of great people management abilities.

So, to me at least, it is obvious that there is very high incentive for each one of you to improve your people management skills and become the best that you can be at it. Be the best leader and the best manager that you can be. It will amplify all the other capabilities you have and grow your career significantly.

Strengthening the 'People' focus and management

Despite this, the interesting thing that I have noticed is that most people do *not* make a conscious effort to grow their people management capabilities to become better managers and leaders. I once had an interesting discussion with some others about why they did not choose to work on improving their people management skills. The broad conclusion we drew was that most people thought that people management is a natural capability and hence improves by itself; one does not have to work on it deliberately. It is something like being a good friend; most of us would not go out of our way to attend a training programme or read a book on how to be a better friend. We assume that the capability to be a good friend develops naturally and does not take any special efforts. Similarly, for most people, the assumption is that people management capability, leadership capability and managerial capability develop naturally. There is some truth to it, it is somewhat of a natural capability. If you want to learn a new computer programming language, just sitting and doing what you do every day won't help. You need to take lessons or read a book or have a colleague teach you. In the case of people management, however, there is a natural aspect and we do learn how to be leaders and managers in a natural way. Part of the skill is driven from our personality and the way we interact with others. As you face challenges with people in your career, you are likely to learn from those experiences quite naturally as well.

However, just relying on the natural process without taking any deliberate actions to improve your people management capabilities can create two challenges:

1. Allowing yourself to improve naturally over time is not a standardized or controlled process. It works differently for different people, and for many people out there, the natural process might not be sufficient to make them the best leaders and managers. Like the natural process does not make everyone great at friendship, it is not necessary that the natural process will make everyone a good leader and manager. Many a time, it might not.

2. The natural process would not be enough to take you to your full potential as a leader and a manager.

It might not be enough to maximize your capability and your impact in that space.

Many organizations and some individuals have realized that there is an opportunity to accelerate the development of leadership and managerial capabilities through deliberate interventions over and above the natural process. Companies do organize leadership development programmes for their talent. Individuals often rely on books to grow themselves, particularly as leaders. There is, however, not so much focus on growing as managers. In most cases, I believe that both company-led interventions and individual efforts do not necessarily lead to good results and acceleration of leadership and managerial capabilities of people. The reason for that is something that I have mentioned in my book *Get Better at Getting Better.* It is related to one of the biggest barriers to learning which is the myth that 'knowing is equal to changing and improving'. Basically, we tend to assume that if we have acquired some new knowledge or learnt a new concept, then just because we know it, we are also practising it. It has become a part of our behaviour. That is incorrect.

Let me give you a few examples for this. There was a research study conducted with a set of professors of ethics. The hypothesis was that since they were professors of ethics, and they had all the knowledge related to ethics, it was likely that their behaviour was more ethical than professors of other subjects. The research study, subject to its limitations, broadly concluded that such was not the case. Just because the ethics professors had more knowledge about ethics did not mean that they were more ethical than other professors. Knowledge is not equal to practice and behaviours. *Similarly, just because you have more knowledge about leadership through reading books and attending leadership programmes, this does not mean you are a better leader. You simply have more knowledge, that's all.* It takes deliberate practice to convert knowledge into behaviour and embed it within. It will not happen by itself. My favourite analogy to communicate this point is that of reading a book on health. Just reading a book and becoming aware of the knowledge contained within does not make you healthier. To become healthier, you have to practise what is written in the book. Deliberate practice to embed that new knowledge is what creates benefit.

When it comes to people management, I see the same tendency—many people attend programmes, online courses, read books on leadership, etc. and then they stop there. There is not enough focus on converting the knowledge they have acquired through deliberate practice into behaviour and capabilities. With this book, I don't want you to make that mistake. I want you to spend time and energy in deliberately practising the concepts covered in this book so that you permanently gain from reading this book and permanently become a better leader and manager. *In fact, my strong recommendation is that you do not read any more leadership books for the next twelve months. Just spend the next twelve months in deliberate practice of what you learnt in this book.* You will gain a lot more by doing that than by reading another five books.

Putting this book into practice

I have been deliberate about how I have written this book, such that it enables you to put it into practice.

I have done two things:

1. From the thousands of leadership and managerial concepts that exist, I have pruned and prioritized down to six concepts that you can practise and master. So, it is a manageable number.
2. I have tried to write down each of the concepts to the best of my ability in a way that it is practical and actionable and not just theoretical. I have not just described the concept, but have also tried to talk about how to build the ability to practise that concept and how to use it.

I am going to put down a practice programme for you based on what you learnt in this book. My sincere request to you would be to implement the practice programme rigorously if you truly want to become a better leader and manager. It can help you chart out career success going forward. The practice programme has two broad areas:

1. Foundation blocks
2. Practising the concepts

Getting the foundation blocks ready

To set the foundation for the practice ahead, you must complete the two foundation blocks—self-awareness, and stakeholders and outcomes.

Self-awareness

Self-awareness is the foundation step before you can start practising the concepts of leading and managing. It is about rooting ourselves and knowing where we stand today. I recommend that you do the following steps to improve your self-awareness as a leader and manager.

1. Complete the ideal boss visualization exercise and also assess how much of that you practise for your team already (from Chapter 2). This should open your eyes to the gap between what you want your boss to do and what you actually do for your team. In a way, you may be choosing to be a less-than-ideal boss for your team.

2. I would also ask you to go to the self-awareness section on page 231 and answer the three questions articulated there:

   a. *What do others think about you?* To answer this question, you can use the various feedbacks you have received over the years, be it in appraisals or otherwise. This is also the time to pull out all your past 360s and analyse them in detail to try and arrive at a good view of what others think of you.

   b. *What do you think of yourself?* Again, 360s can be good sources of this information, since most 360s also ask you to evaluate yourself. This question is essentially about your self-image: who do you think you are?

   c. *Who are you really? Who are you at the core?* This is about peeling the onion to know who you really are. Your self-image of who you think you are could often be wishful thinking of what you want to be, not what you really are. Answer the question of who you are at the core with the help of some of the tips I have given on page 231 to 233 and your own reflection.

At the end of the self-awareness exercise, you should have four sheets of paper: one page for each of the above points, starting from the ideal boss visualization exercise to who you really are at the core. Please be as honest as possible while doing this exercise. You need to be genuinely self-aware and not live in a make-believe world. At the same time, do not be overly self-critical. We are looking for truth here, and whether it is good or bad is not important at this stage because whatever it may be, we are going to improve it further through our practice.

Stakeholders and outcomes

This is about understanding who the stakeholders are to us as leaders and managers. Who are the people who have an interest in the outcomes we deliver as leaders and managers and who are those who are impacted by our actions as leaders and managers? To do this, you have to complete the exercise from Chapter 3, Page 47, on mapping who your stakeholders are and the outcomes that they expect from you. Please do this mapping exercise using specific names for stakeholders wherever possible as that will prevent you from being generic in articulating outcomes. Think of a name, think of that person, and then ask yourself what that person expects from you as a leader and manager. This is not a KRA sheet or an annual goal sheet exercise. It focuses on outcomes expected from you as a leader and manager, and not all outcomes from you as a role holder such as financial results and business performance, etc. Once you've completed this mapping, use the assessment process given in Chapter 3, Page 47 to evaluate yourself on how good you are at meeting stakeholder outcomes.

Understanding all stakeholders and outcomes is truly vital to becoming a good leader and manager. This helps you understand if you are leading and managing only for some stakeholders and a few outcomes, i.e., whether you are a holistic leader or not. It is very important to become a holistic leader to get to the very top of organizations in your career.

Both self-awareness and mapping stakeholders and expected outcomes are important foundation blocks to prepare for the practice of concepts to become a good leader and manager. This will help you realize where you are right now and also what is expected of you as a leader and manager. Please do not start the practice without completing the foundation steps.

Practising concepts regularly

Truth be told, by serendipity, my understanding about the power of practice in growing people as leaders and managers got amplified thanks to the COVID lockdown and the work-from-home model. Before the lockdown, when I used to run the 'Lead & Manage' programme for a company, I would run it over two days and then bank on people having the self-discipline after that to practise and apply concepts. Thanks to the lockdown, I changed the design of the programme. Instead of running it over two days back-to-back, the new design has six sessions of three hours each with significant gaps after each session for the participants to actually practise the concepts in their real world and come back with the learning of having applied it for a discussion in the next session. I am convinced that this design will create even greater learning than an end-to-end two-day programme. The two-day programme was necessitated when it was conducted physically at a single location with participants often travelling from across cities to attend. While they can't travel six times for a single programme, in a WFH world where people are participating from their laptops wherever they are, travel and logistics constraints are removed. This enables a more powerful programme design which ensures practice and learning by application.

To enable the practice, as I mentioned before, I have been quite brutal in prioritizing six concepts for you to learn and practise to become a good leader and manager. On the topic of leadership alone, there are possibly 10,000+ books and an unknown number of concepts. If we further add what it takes to be a good manager, then the count of concepts you have to learn and practise is unmanageable. I have used personal experience and my observation of others to narrow it down to six concepts that you can actually practise and master. I am also quite confident that if you master those six, you would be well on your way to transforming into a great leader and manager.

The six critical concepts

The six concepts that I have prioritized for you are categorized as follows:

1. PAMOD—Managing for performance
2. Ability-Motivation matrix (AM)—Managing the performer
   (These first two are for managing **individuals** who report directly to you.)
3. Delegation
4. Creating amplifying teams
   (The next two are for creating effectiveness in **teams** that are reporting directly to you.)
5. Leading by doing—VISA
6. Leading by being—Value-based leadership, behaviour towards people and role modelling
   (The last two concepts are for having a **wider impact in the organization**—beyond the people and teams you manage directly.)

Put together, these six concepts give you mastery over the entire gamut of skills required for being a great leader and manager—all the way from managing an individual to having widespread impact across the entire company and even outside, at times.

The four blocks from the six concepts

For purposes of practice, I have condensed these six concepts into four blocks.

Block 1: PAMOD and AM matrix
Block 2: Delegation and creation of amplifying teams
Block 3: Leading by doing—VISA
Block 4: Leading by being

There are two reasons why I have condensed these into four blocks:

1. Some of the concepts are mutually complementary and address the same area. For example, both PAMOD and AM matrix are about managing individuals, and there is value in practising them together.
2. Earlier in the chapter, I had requested you to set aside twelve months for practising and mastering these concepts and not to read any further books till you finish this practice. The reason I break this into four blocks is because my estimate is that it will take three months for you to practise each block. Hence, the four blocks will take a year.

Creating a practice programme

Assuming that you are now sold on people management, and want to become a great leader and manager, you are ready to start the practice in that direction. So let us now build the practice programme.

The first and the most important thing is that you have to practise one block at a time for three months each. Trying to do two or three blocks at the same time will not work and will not give you good results. That is because each block requires focus and multiple repetitions of practice and iterative learning. So, you have to choose one block for a period of three months and be single-minded about it.

This then brings us to the next question: what is the right sequence to practise the blocks in? Should we do block one for the first three months, block two for the next three and so on or can we be flexible with the order? I do recommend that if you are comfortable, please progress as per the natural progression of starting with block one and ending with block four over twelve months. But, at times, individuals may feel more attracted to one block over another; they might feel they will gain more by going out of sequence and practising and applying one of the later blocks earlier in the cycle. I am not against that. That has its own benefits provided you are doing it with sound logic and not based on just a vague feeling. Different people are in different contexts—some are senior, some are junior, some feel they have already mastered some of the concepts and want to focus on where they feel they have more to learn; some have very effective direct teams while others don't have equally effective direct teams, etc. Hence, based on different individual contexts, there can be a different sequence to practising the blocks and concepts.

I would, however, not recommend that you be random about the sequence. It must be tied to your context. I recommend the framework below to help you decide the sequence in which you can practise the concepts. On the Y axis is your seniority—how senior a leader you are. This is based on where you are in the organizational hierarchy, not based on your age. The higher you are up the organizational ladder, the more senior you are. On the X axis is the effectiveness of the team directly reporting to you—how effective are they in their functioning. Based on which quadrant you are, you can choose the sequence of practice as recommended for that quadrant.

		Low	High
High		PAMOD AM matrix Leading by Doing Delegation Amplifying teams Leading by Being	Leading by Doing Leading by Being Delegation Amplifying teams PAMOD AM matrix
Low		PAMOD AM matrix Delegation Amplifying teams Leading by Doing Leading by Being	Delegation Amplifying teams PAMOD AM matrix Leading by Doing Leading by Being

Seniority (Y axis)

Effectiveness of direct team

I do want to emphasize here that this is about the sequence for practising the concepts. This is not about their relative importance. There are only six concepts in total and all are important. We are trying to build our capabilities in three areas—managing individuals, managing direct teams and creating impact in the wider organization. Each of these three areas only has two concepts against it. Hence, if you are weak in the practice of even one concept, then you are possibly going to be weak in that area. So please give equal importance to all the concepts, even if you choose to sequence your practice based on what is most appropriate for your context.

Now, let us get to the actual practice. Let us say you are in the first phase of three months and have chosen to practise PAMOD and AM matrix in this period. Here is how I recommend you progress in that practice:

1. In week one, read the relevant chapters at least three times each. Your goal should be to know the contents of the chapter at least as well as I know them. Reading a chapter does not take more than thirty–forty minutes. Hence, four hours should be sufficient to read both chapters thrice.

2. In week two, make a practice plan for each concept. In each chapter, I have provided steps on how to practise and learn the concept. I don't want to repeat it here. What you need to do is to build a plan where each of those steps has a week and date against it. You can also modify the steps or add to the steps I have given, if necessary.

3. Weeks three–six form the first cycle of practice based on the plan you have made.

4. Week seven is about interim review. Review for yourself how you are progressing, what is working well, what is not working well, how comfortable you are getting in internalizing and applying the concepts, etc. Based on this interim review, change your practice plan for the next six weeks, if required.

5. Weeks seven–twelve are all about the practice as per the revised plan you have made.
6. Week twelve–thirteen is the final review where you assess what are you doing well, what can be better, how comfortable you are with the concepts, if you feel that they are now a part of you, etc. If at this stage you feel that there is a need for more practice, extend the practice by one month—the twelve months can become thirteen.

I cannot overemphasize how important it is to adhere to your practice plans, to have the discipline and motivation to execute them and truly develop as a better leader and manager. It is very frustrating to watch so many people fall into the 'knowing is equal to improving' trap. Without practising the knowledge that you have, you have not improved or become a better leader. *Reading this book is the starting point to becoming a better leader and manager, not the end point. The end point is when you have practised the concepts and they become a part of your daily behaviour—they are a part of you.*

The practice of concepts associated with leading and managing is particularly challenging because they don't result in short-term gains. If you start today, nothing spectacular will happen tomorrow. These are gradual processes of changing and improving yourself. Because of the lack of short-term benefits, many people quickly give up the practice and lose the determination to stay the course. To help motivate you, I want to go to the 'hare and the tortoise story', where the steady tortoise beats the fast hare in a race. The oft-quoted moral of the story is 'slow and steady wins the race'. I want to give you a slightly different take: 'focused and steady wins the race'. The hare lost because it was not focused on the end goal; it was not getting enough excitement in the race, not enough short-term gratification, and so it got distracted and dozed off. The tortoise won because it was focused on the end goal and took one step at a time towards that goal, even if each step was not exciting. Keep that image of the tortoise—who is goal-focused and takes one step at a time without losing the determination and the focus, without wondering how he benefitted from that one step—in your mind. The lesson isn't to be slow like a tortoise—there is nothing wrong with being fast, as long as you stay focused on the end goal and maintain the determination of the tortoise to stay the course till you reach it. Remember, that end goal for you is becoming a great leader and manager. You have to keep at it till then.

An important question: What is your real legacy?

In the companies I have worked in, I do feel I made some fundamental impact. I left those companies better because I worked there. Many others who worked in those companies have also done that. So, how should I think about the legacy I left behind in those companies?

One way is to think of the lasting positive contributions I made to those companies. I could think of how I helped Asian Paints become strong in Royale, when as a brand manager, I changed the strategy from being competitor-focused to one that was based on category expansion. Or for that matter how I helped Asian Paints evolve from an interior paints company to an interior as well as exterior paints company. I could think of how at Onida, the time when I was there coincided with the entry of LG and Samsung into India. While a much larger Indian company—BPL—could not stand up to their competition and folded, Onida stood strong and survived that storm and remained a growing and profitable company through that phase. I could think of that as my legacy there. At Mondelez, I could think of how before I took up HR, Cadbury was a strong consumer brand but not at the top as an employer brand on campuses. In a few years, I took it from day three/four to day zero/one in premium management campuses and fundamentally changed the talent attraction capability of the company. I could think about getting Mondelez into biscuits as my legacy. At Pidilite, I could think of how I got a conventional company engaged in the start-up ecosystem by making a set of strategic investments. Each of the above are positive contributions I made, and I could be justified in thinking of these as my legacies.

But there is an interesting counterpoint—no one in those companies today thinks too much of these contributions I made. In all probability, most people in those companies don't even know I existed, and that I made a difference. I don't blame them for that. That is how life is and that is how even I was. When I was there in those companies, I did not go out of my way to find out what difference someone who worked a decade before me made. Why should I expect any different now when it concerns my legacy? In short, the point I am trying to make is that when you think of your legacy in terms of contributions you made; the new products you launched;

the factory or BPO you set up from scratch; the new IT system you embedded into the company, etc., they remain only in your mind. They are forgotten by the world and those companies fairly quickly.

But there is one legacy which, if you leave, does not get forgotten easily. And that the positive impact you have created on the people in your time in that company. I found that while all the business contributions I made to the various companies got forgotten easily, the people whom I had positively impacted as a leader and manager; the people who grew as professionals and as human beings because of me, have not forgotten me. They are in regular touch with me wherever they are in the world and are appreciative of the fact that as their leader and manager, I made a positive difference to them even a few decades down the line. I still get messages from my Asian Paints marketing team, and if they happen to pass by Mumbai, they try and meet me, and we often exchange pleasant, nostalgic memories. My Onida team—with whom I worked seventeen years ago—still loves me and respects me for the difference I made to them. Recently, I got a message from one of them saying that he believes his entire career success was because of the learning he got from working under me in Onida. I am sure that is an exaggeration, but the point is he remembers me for what difference I made to him, not for which new TV models I launched and how successful they were. And so is the case with the people at Cadbury/Mondelez who I worked with. People all around India and outside, in Mondelez and other companies, who are in constant touch with me and care for me, love me and I love them as well. All these people are my true legacy.

So, if you are lacking in determination and the motivation required to put in the work to become a better leader and manager, this is the final motivating argument I want to leave you with. Your legacy will not be the business contributions you made; the financial results you delivered; the services and products and the software you launched. All that will be forgotten by everyone else except you. But become a great leader and manager, impact people positively; make them better professionally and as human beings and they will never forget that. They will not forget it even when you forget it, and that is the true legacy you will leave. God bless you for wanting to become a great leader, a great manager and for wanting to leave people better off.

A final word

In conclusion, I feel this book is my gift to all you people who are reading it—my dear readers. In my lifetime, I have seen the amazing power of connecting with and impacting people, and I want you to exercise that power in your life at work. The overall impact of learning to deal with people well is going to be the best investment you will ever make in your career. You will then not only be able to manage them, but truly lead them—and you will always be amazed at the wonderful returns of that.

We all recognize the power of human relationships in our personal life, but at work, we often miss out on it. This book is a reminder that whether it is our personal life, or work life, people matter. And the more we learn about that, our lives will become more successful—successful beyond just the usual markers of success. We will always live on in people's minds and hearts, way beyond our job, designation and organization—way beyond just the work that we did together.

I wish you that wonderful space in your work and in your life, through this book.

Acknowledgements

Writing the acknowledgements for this book has been the most difficult part for me. It really does signal the end of an era in a way, with the completion and release of this book by my father, Chandramouli Venkatesan.

During this year-long endeavour, which will continue for the next few months, there are so many people who have supported me in getting this book to you, the reader. In a way, I have been shown the power of my father's own personal practice of everything he teaches in this book. He had a huge network of family, friends, colleagues and readers in his lifetime who supported me purely out of their appreciation for him—as a person, as a writer and as a corporate leader. So, I begin with an enormous sense of gratitude for being blessed with a father like him—who taught me in the time we had together, by sheer example, what it means to live a meaningful life. He created a much larger family for me to turn to, when he would no longer be there. Without all the things he achieved in his life, this book would not have been possible—not just in terms of writing the content, but also in getting it out there to the world.

Over the year, I have inherited a much larger 'family', and I have to express my gratitude to them. To Alka and Bharat Puri, I really have no words other than the sincerest thanks to offer—for the sheer simplicity with which I have been adopted into your lives and the absolute confidence I now have in knowing that I always have you on my side. Thanks as well to Sukanya and Anand Kripalu, who have stayed and supported me and my family in what has been a very complicated year. Huge thanks to the entire 'Celebrating Mouli' group—some of the closest people in his network who made it a point to ensure I always had someone to turn to, no matter what issue may arise. I'm sure there are so many more people in his network who I don't know well, but who have helped him and provided their invaluable support through his journey from *Catalyst* to *Transform*. Thank you, all of you friends and supporters.

I am very grateful for the constant support of Radhika Marwah, who has not just been an amazing editor, but a true personal supporter for this book. Also, thanks to the entire team at Penguin Random House for their support at different stages of the book. It made the whole process much easier.

I would like to thank Sam Balsara, chairman, Madison World, as well as his team, for their support in marketing and PR all through the earlier two books, as well as for *Transform*. Also, special thanks to Himanshu Parmekar for his fantastic social media support, and to Animesh Das for being the force behind all the video content for the three books.

It would be amiss if I did not mention my own family, especially my mom and grandfather, who have always been steadfast and supportive of me. Also, Kumar uncle and Prasad uncle, my uncle and aunt—Balaji and Sudha—who have always been there to watch out for me and mom. And finally, to my dear friends—Sharvari, Nilesh, Setu and Monica—thank you for listening to me whine and worry endlessly, and being there whenever I need someone to talk to.

I would like to end this book with a poem excerpt that I think sums it up for me:

'I had an inheritance from my father,
It was the moon and the sun.
And though I roam all over the world,
The spending of it's never done.'
                    —Ernest Hemingway, *For Whom the Bell Tolls*

                              —Prerana Chandramouli